The Diamond & Heart Art Collections

Books by the Anonymous Author and Artist

Duty & Destruction I

A real female experiences life in and out of the U.S. military.

Life's Poetic Dichotomies

Some of life's biggest dichotomies are juxtaposed poetically.

Her Poetic Rise

It is for the religiously poetic that blends religion and feminism.

Life's Short Stories

Fictional characters vie to live their own lives.

Life's Mixed Poetry

Poems are mixed schematically, stylistically, and randomly.

Life's Novellas: Fate Waits Upon No One

The good and the bad are juxtaposed, chronologically, fictionally, and theatrically.

Their Poetic Minds

Poems are juxtaposed, religiously, femininely, and dichotomously.

Poems of Life

Poems are mixed schematically, stylistically, and randomly.

Life's Heart Break: A Novella

In the end, will Zenald discover one of life's biggest heart-breaks: heart-ache?

The Diamond & Heart Art Collections

Anonymous

Century Conquests

The Diamond & Heart Art Collections

Copyright © 2013 by Anonymous

www.centuryconquests.com
info@centuryconquests.com

ISBN: 978-0-9850698-8-9

Cover graphic designed by: Century Conquests © 2013

Century Conquests' Pictures; Photographs; Artwork © 2012; 2013

Century Conquests ® 2012

The Diamond & Heart Art Collections

Anonymous

Acknowledgements

For the small voice deep within me that wants me to carry on, absolutely, artistically.

I thank Microsoft's pretty picture—or, pretty photographic tools;
For its facilitation of this photogenic if not pictorial presentation.

Also, I thank each person that has helped with the publication of this book.

I thank, especially, every person that has indulged this art book.

Introduction

Such art work concerns it-self, in essence, with multi-shaped diamonds and multi-shaped hearts or the very random mixture thereof; whose multi-colors are comprised of five, basic, and categorical shades of coloring: *primary colors*—red, blue, yellow, and so forth; *earth tones*—brown, tan, umber, and so on; *pastels*—aqua, lime, pink, and the like; and even *neutral* or *solid colors*—gray, black, and white; black and white. For the most part, the art work is categorized, further, into those five, main categories, withstanding some mixing of the various coloring.

More, the art work not only has a varied mix of the five, basic, and categorical shades of colors. But, also, it has a varied mix of the most neutral or solid of colors: gray, black, and white; which, right, within themselves comprise sub-categories of such art work. That may very well be entitled: "The Gray, Black & White Diamond & Heart Art Collection"; and, even, "The Black & White Diamond & Heart Art Collection."

Furthermore, to achieve the artistically visual effect as seen in the artistic pictures; the anonymous author and artist; or, I have employed, basically, five, artistic apparatuses: colored pencils; water coloring; pastel coloring; plus, acrylic coloring; and, even, oil coloring; some of which, may very well have been mixed together; all of which, have been so affected with special effects.

What is more, the artistic inspiration for such art work, essentially, has been to create an artistic frame-work; by which its interior showcases certain diamond-shaped designs, and certain heart-shaped designs, among other designs. Or, to have just let the pictures take on lives of their very own, artistically, and, creatively, and, even, figuratively, if not, literally. Or, even, to have just set some internal and external boundaries of some sorts, while simultaneously allowing such boundaries to be crossed—or, super imposed on.

Enjoy!

Artistic beauty is in the arty eyes of the absolutely aspirant artist;
Whose artistry inspires others, artistically, to create his or her own art.

ƒb.

Collection I

Set 1
Pastel Shades
Numbers 1, 2, 3, 4, 5
Colored Pencils & Pastel Coloring & Water Coloring

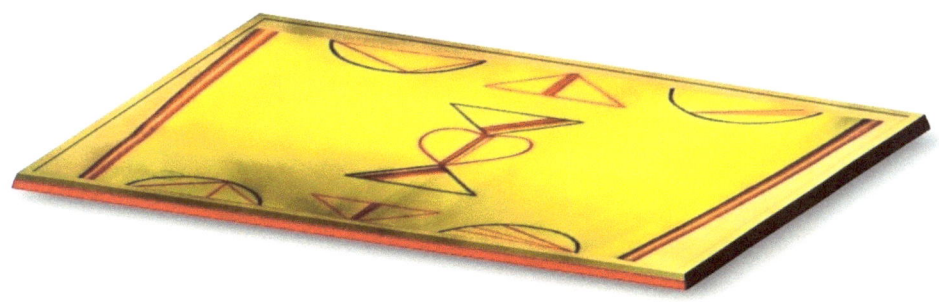

1

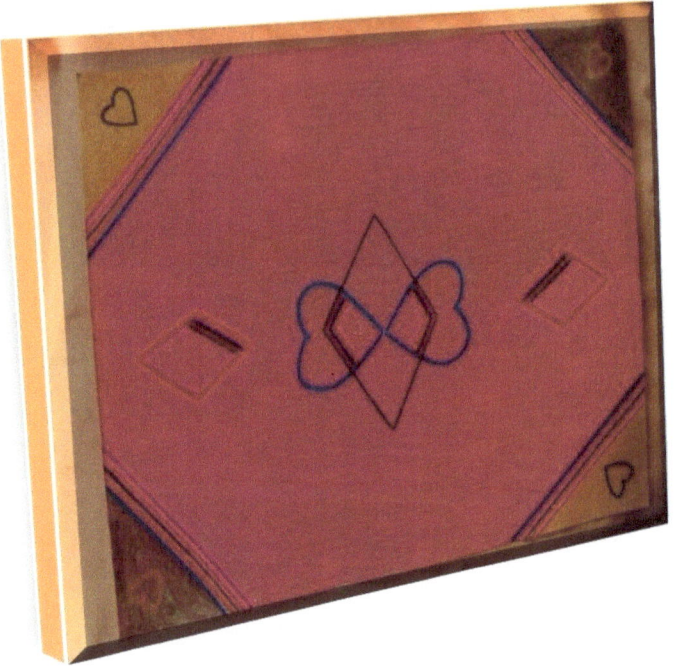

#2

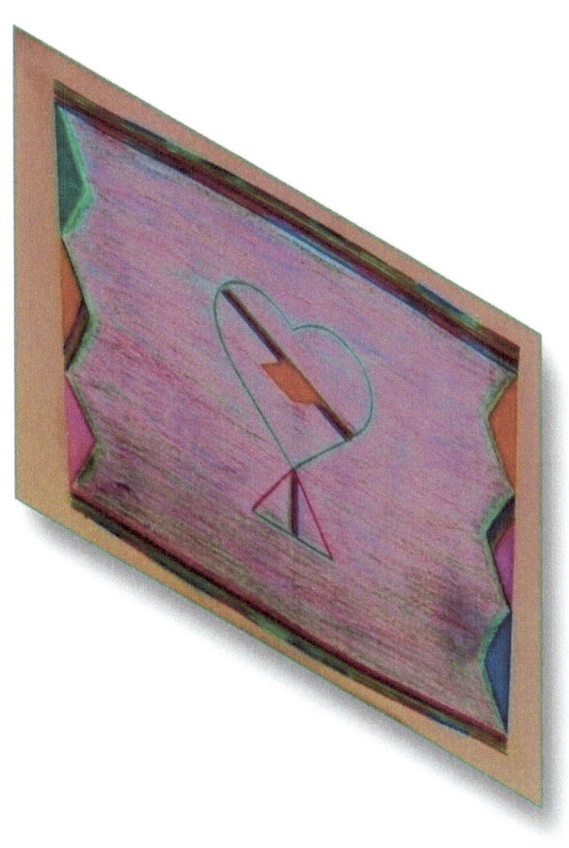

3

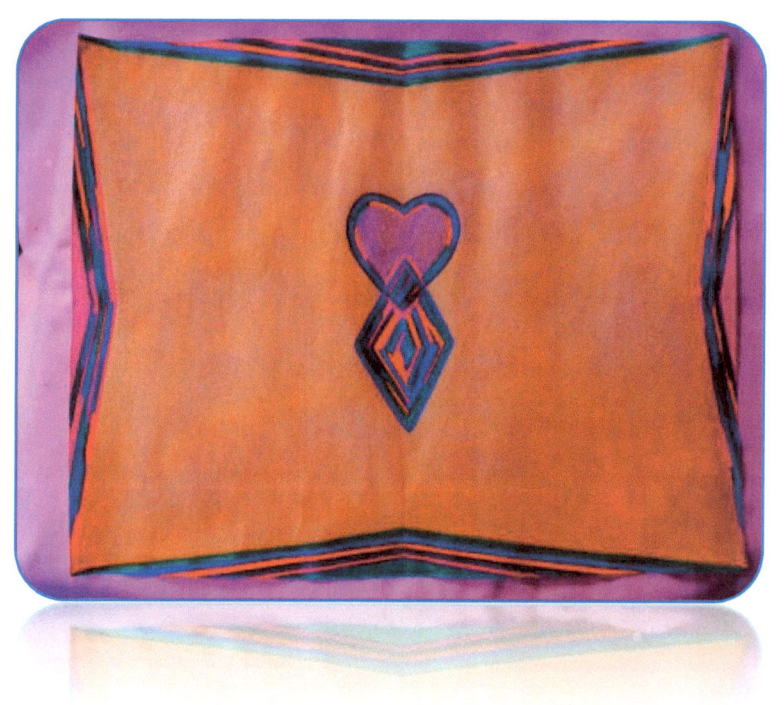

4

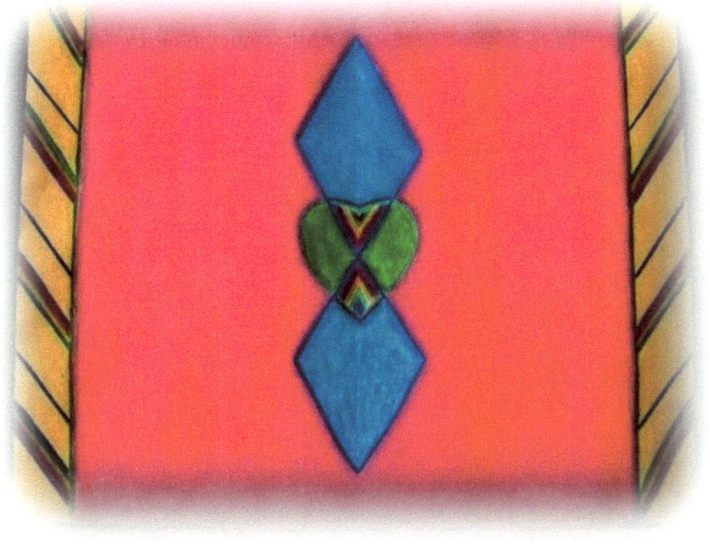

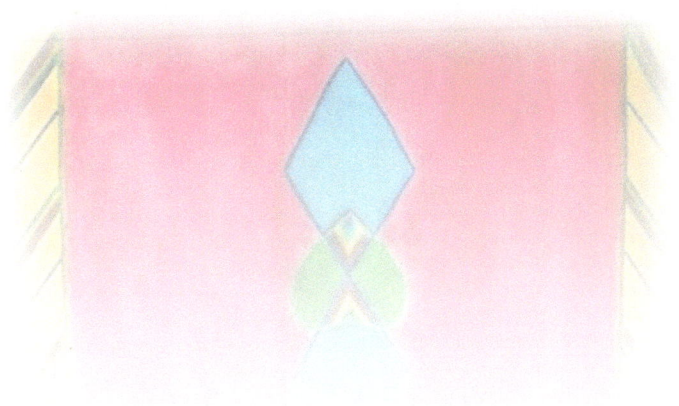

5

Set 2
Earth Tones
Numbers 1, 2, 3, 4, 5
Colored Pencils & Pastel Coloring & Water Coloring

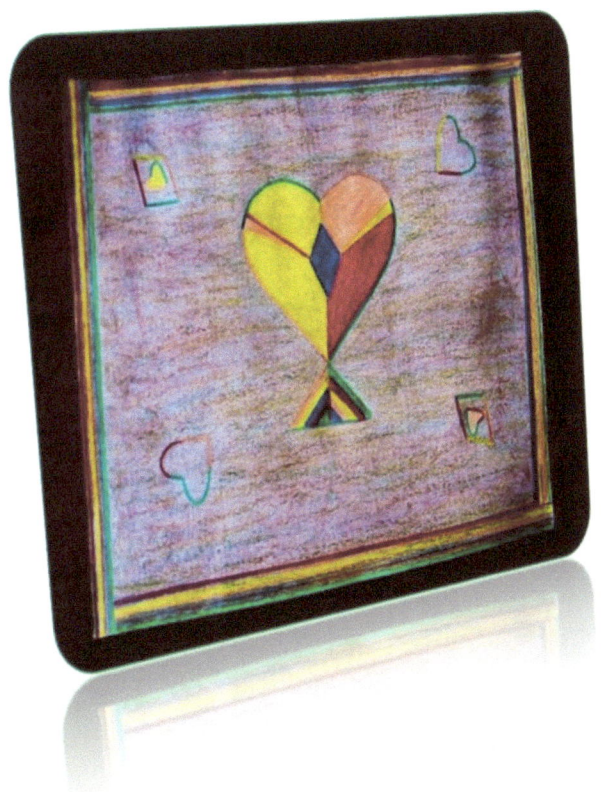

\# 1

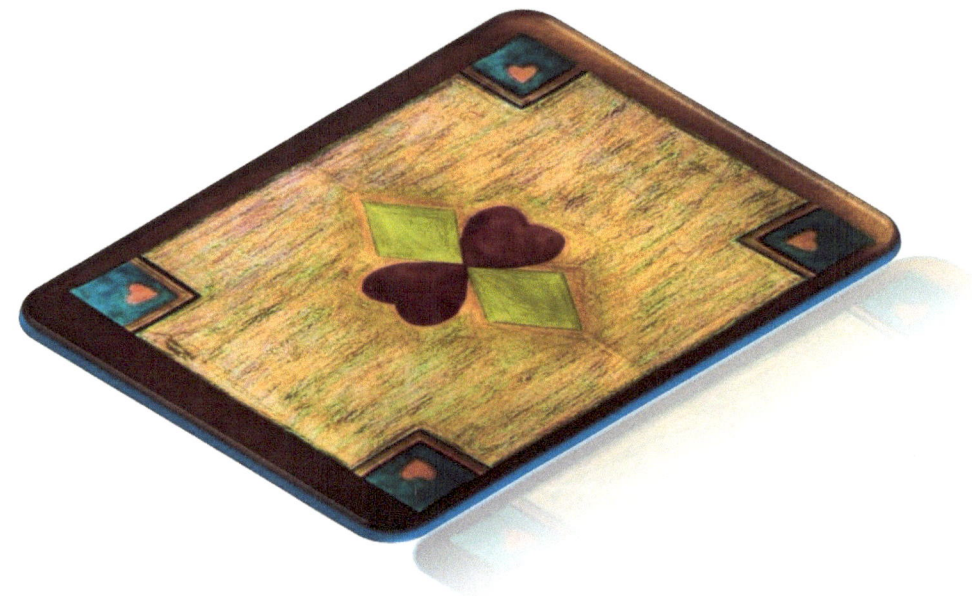

2

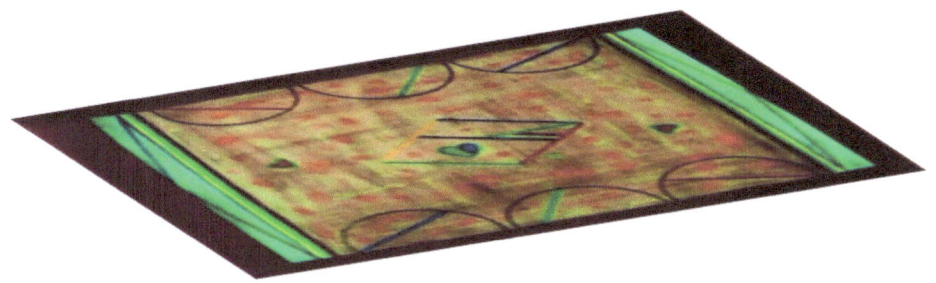

3

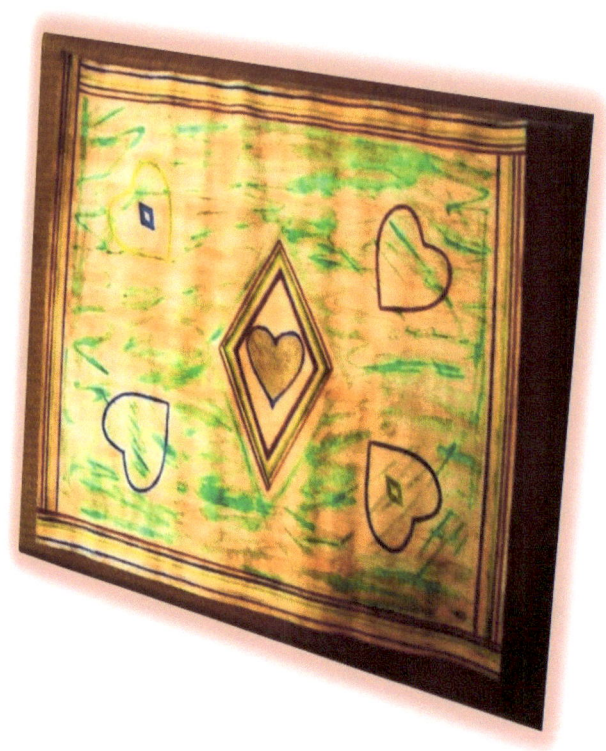

4

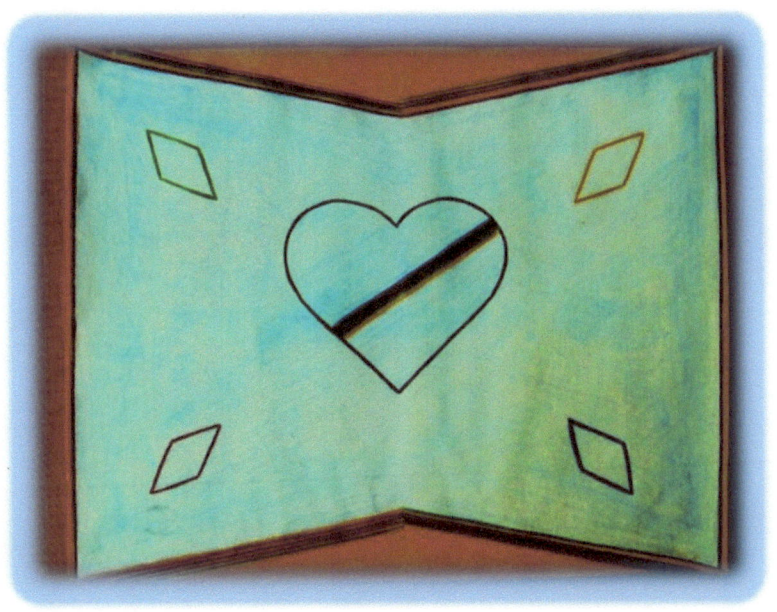

5

Set 3
Primary Colors
Numbers 1, 2, 3, 4, 5
Colored Pencils & Pastel Coloring & Water Coloring

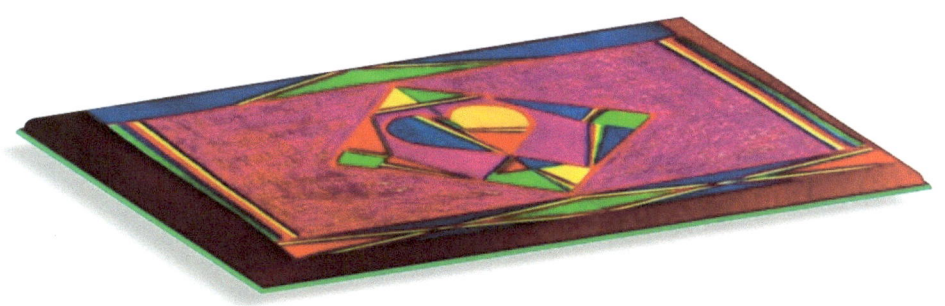

#1

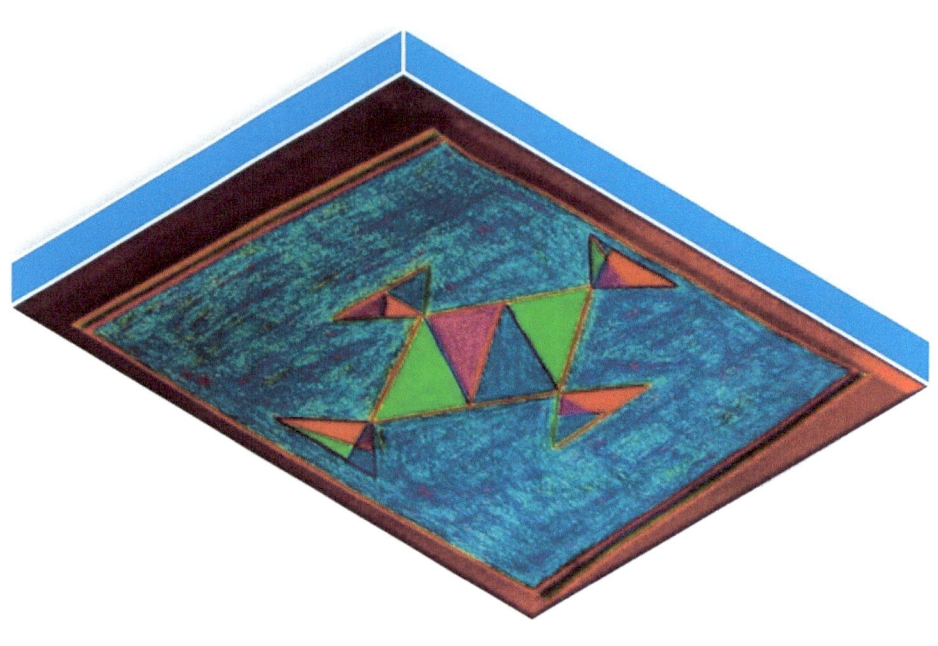

2

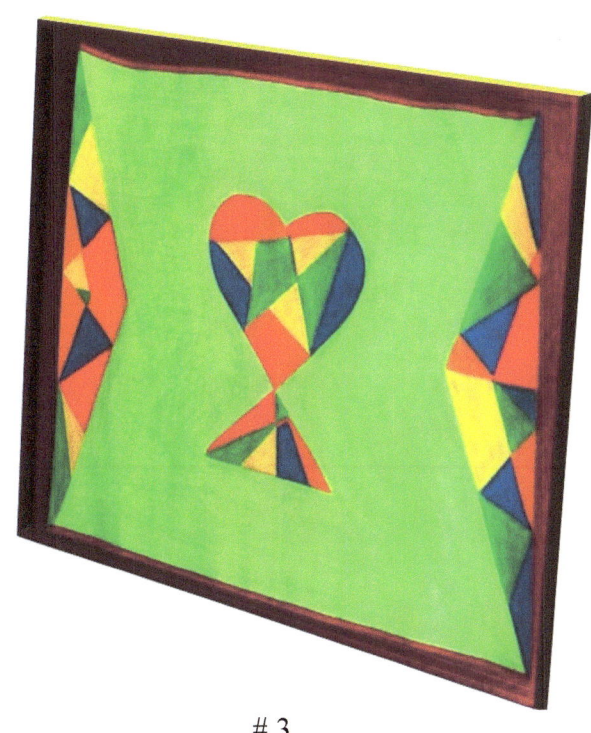

3

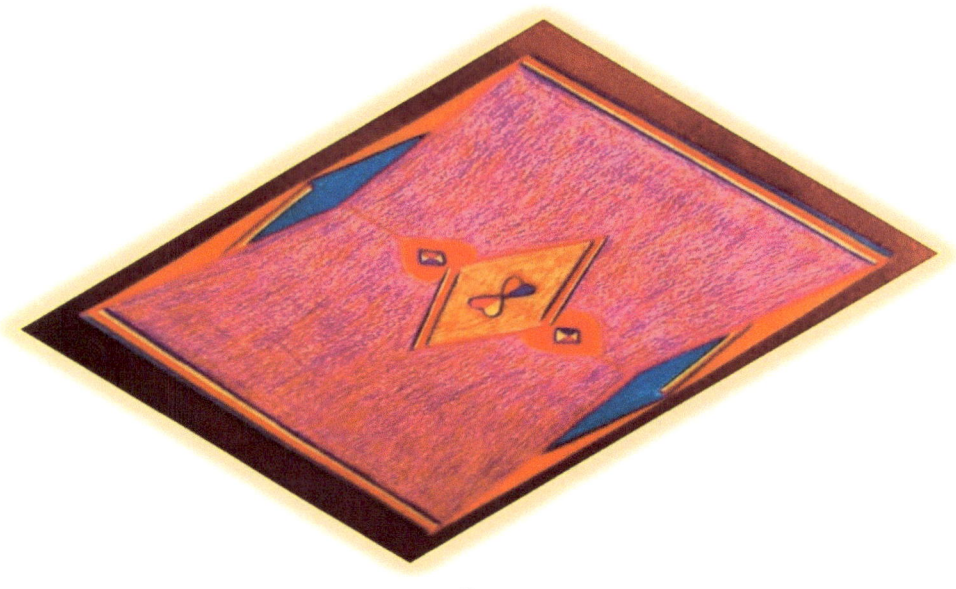

4

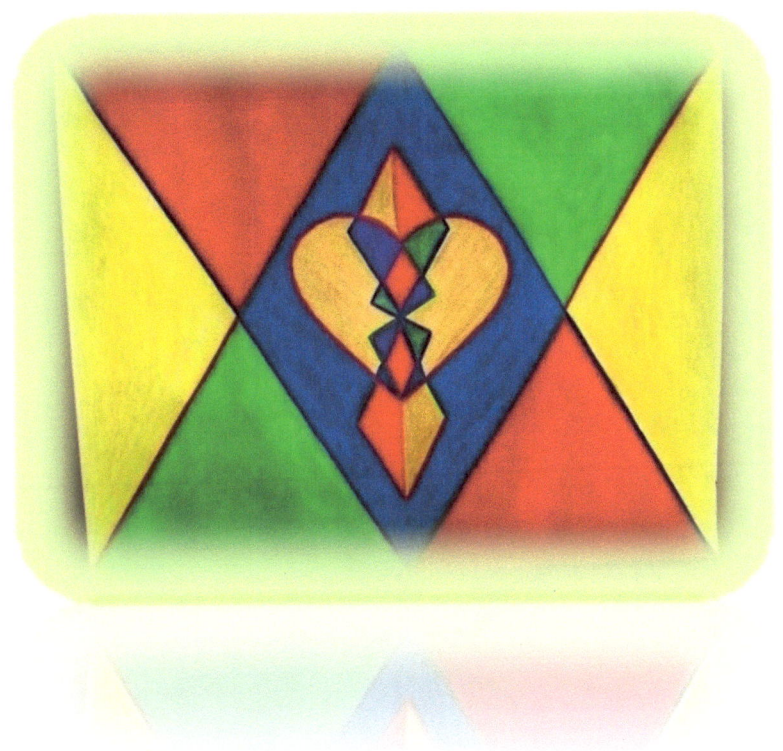

5

Set 4
The Gray, Black & White Diamond & Heart
Art Collection
Numbers 1, 2, 3, 4, 5
Colored Pencils & Pastel Coloring & Water Coloring

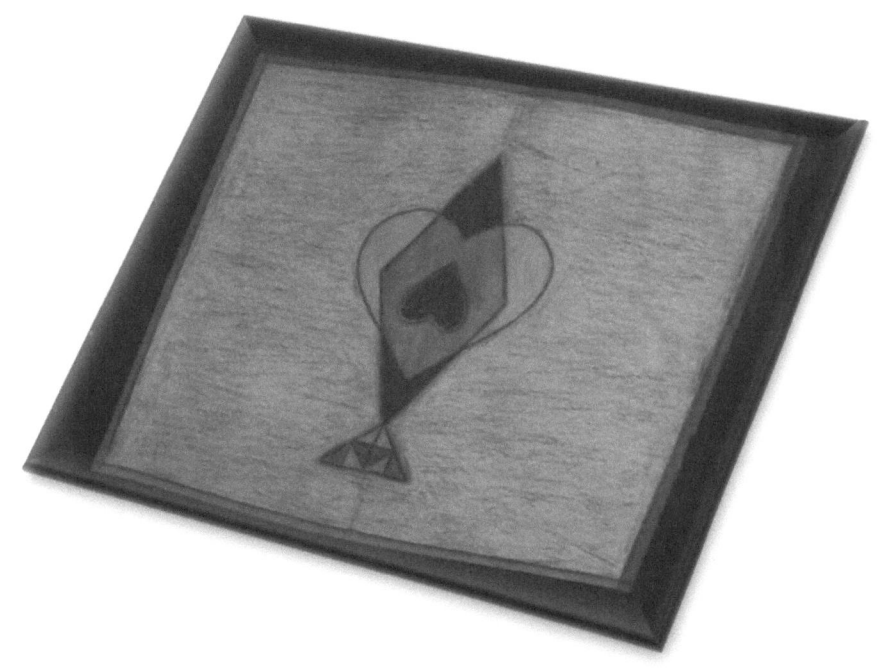

1

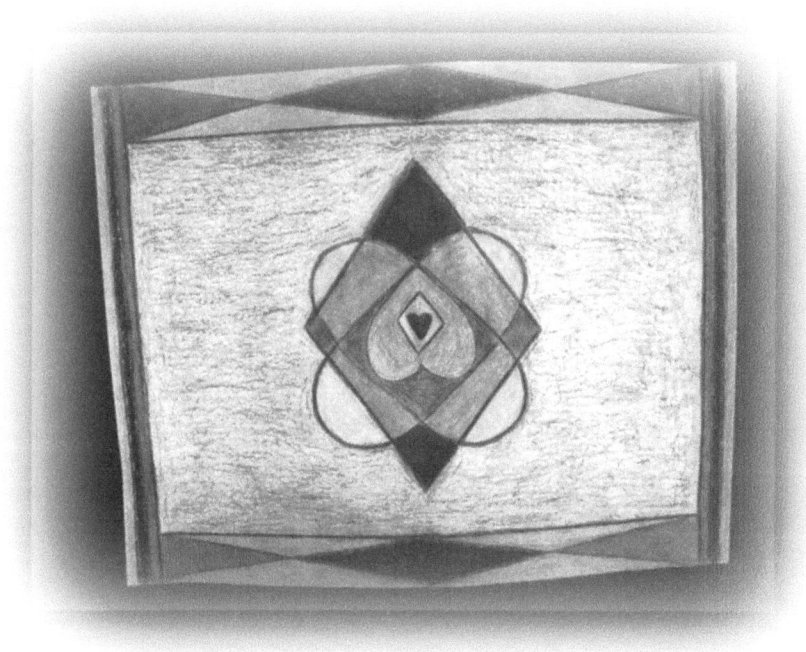

2

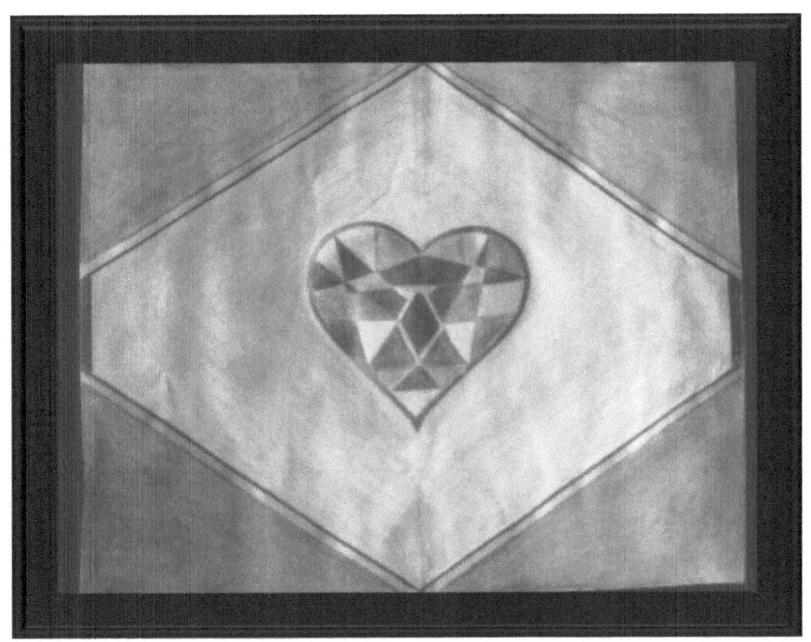

3

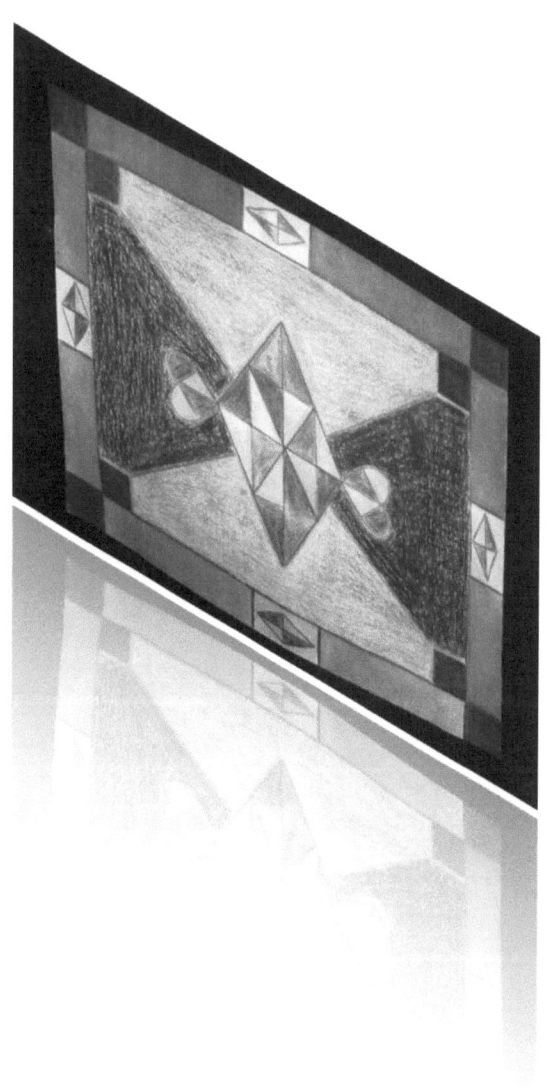

4

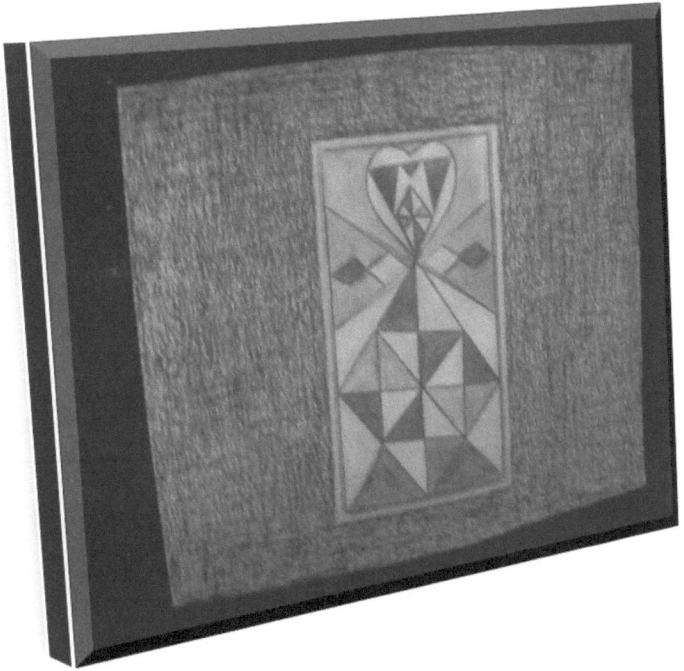

5

Set 5
The Black & White Diamond & Heart Art Collection
Numbers 1, 2, 3, 4, 5
Colored Pencils & Pastel Coloring & Water Coloring

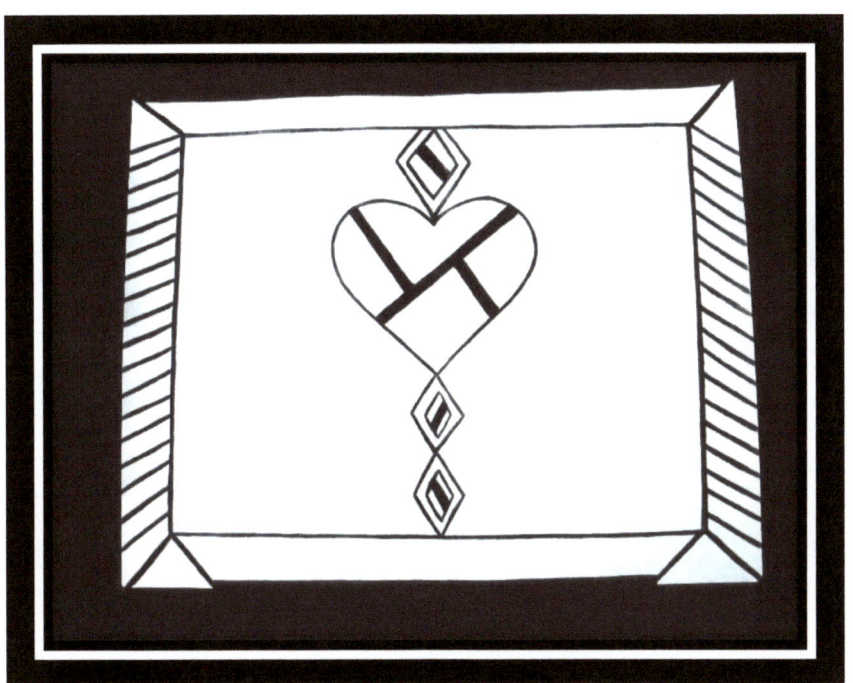

1

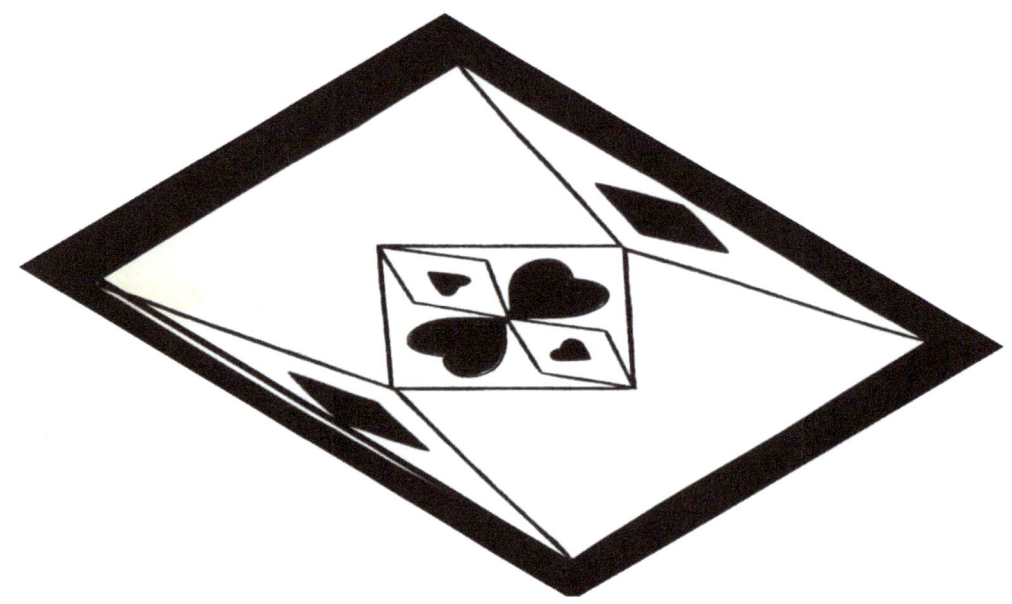

#2

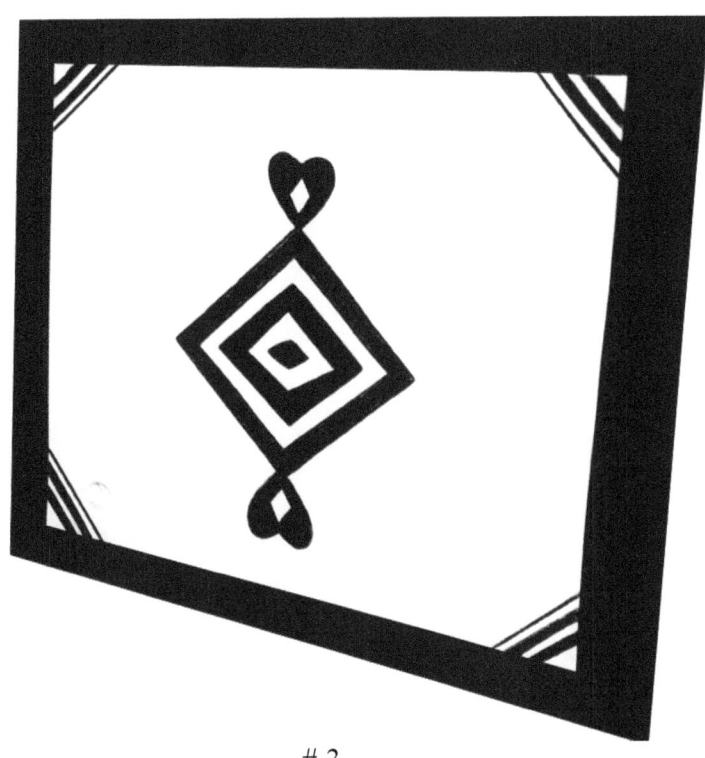

3

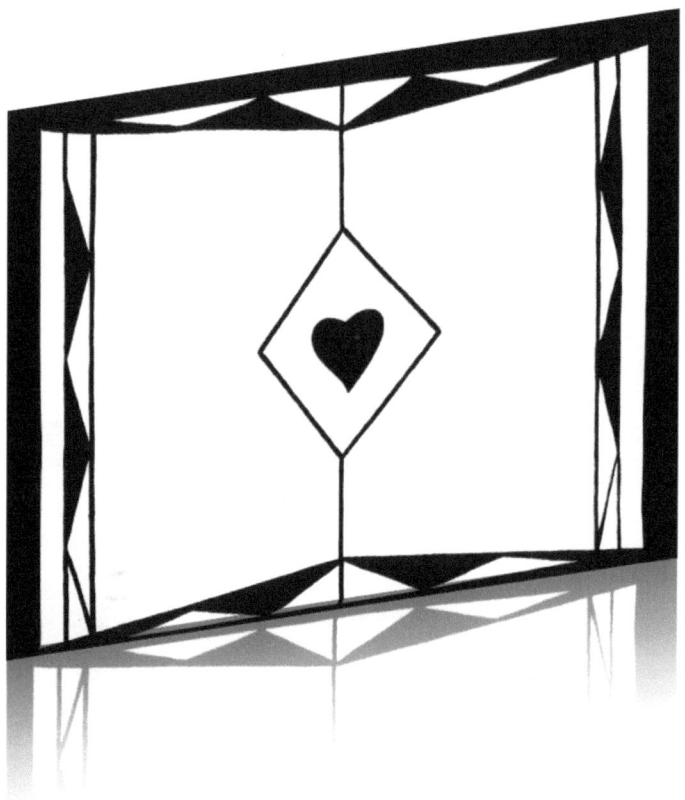

4

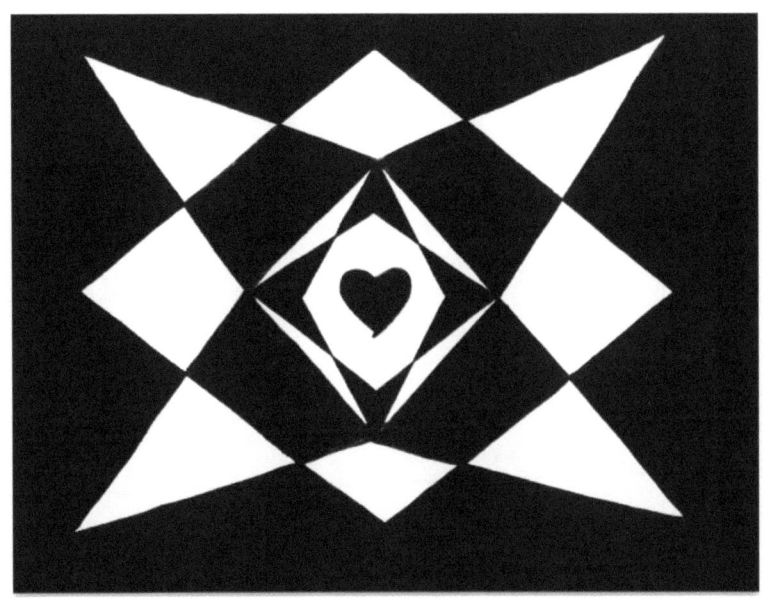

#5

Collection LL

Set 1
Earth Tones
Numbers 1, 2, 3, 4, 5
Colored Pencils & Pastel Coloring & Acrylic Coloring

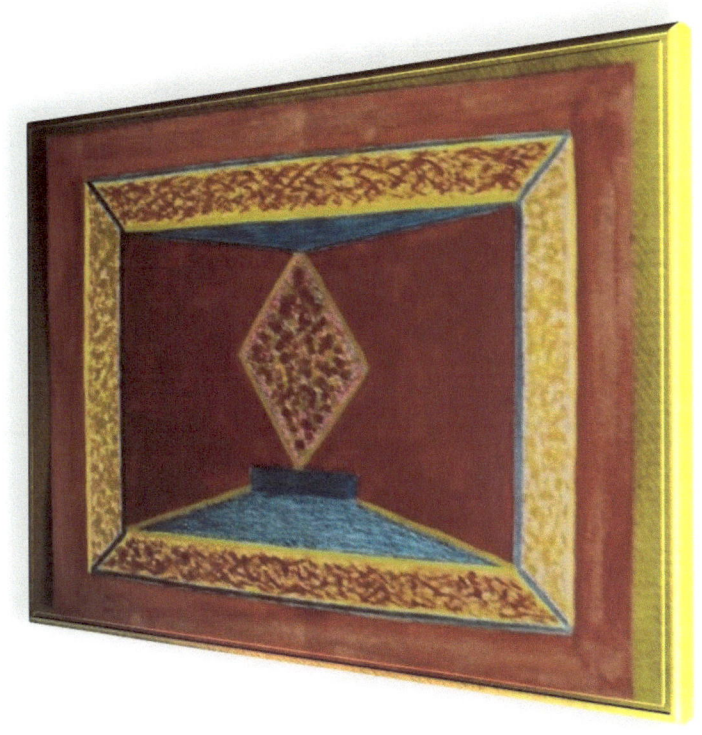

1

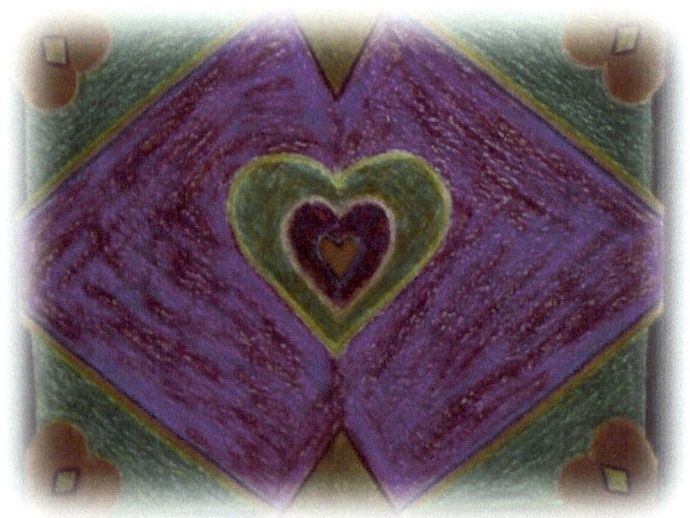

2

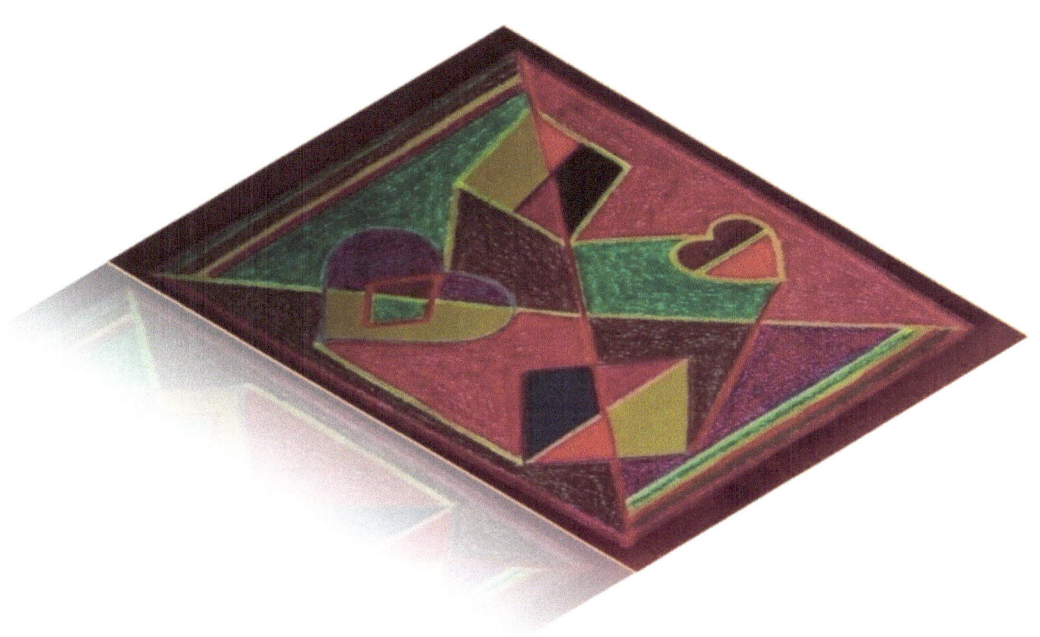

3

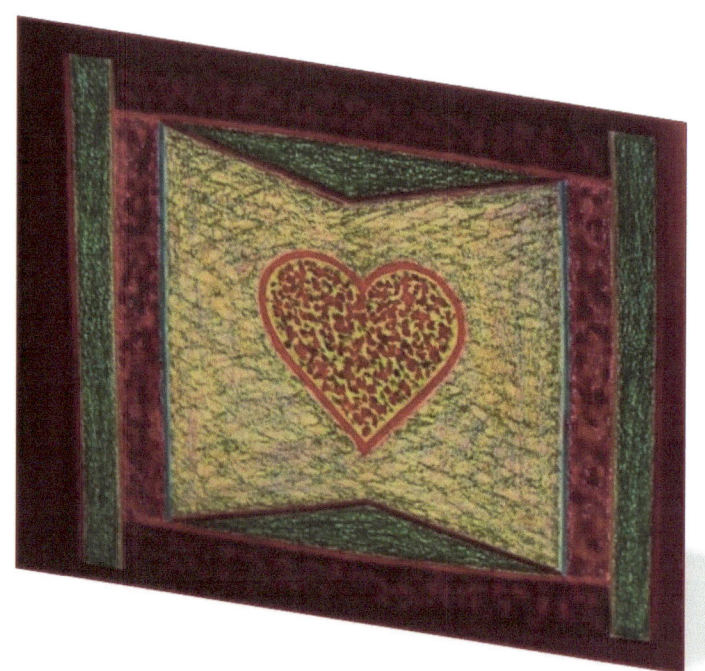

4

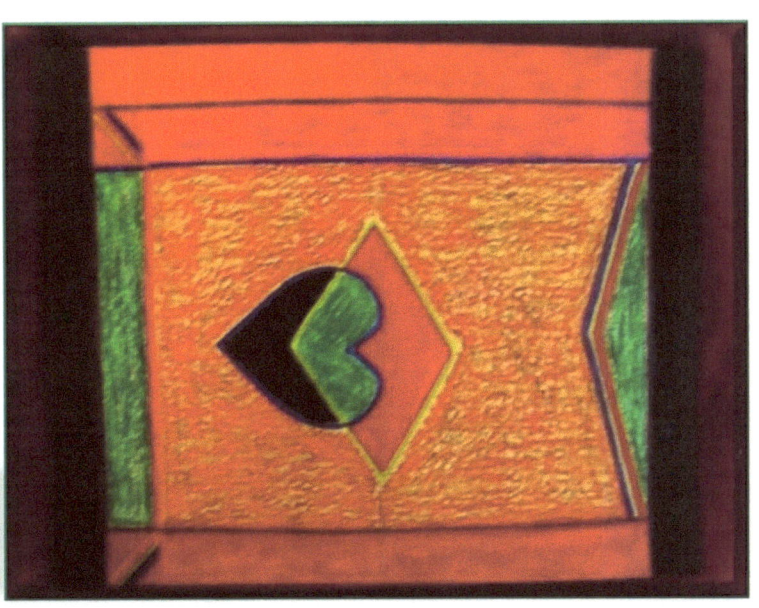

5

Set 2
Primary Colors
Numbers 1, 2, 3, 4, 5
Colored Pencils & Pastel Coloring & Acrylic Coloring

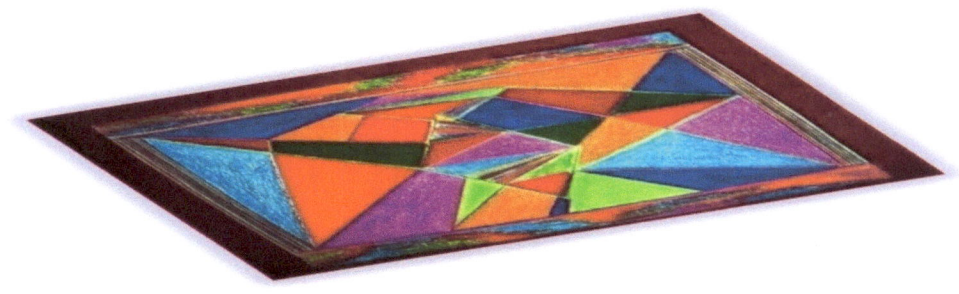

#1

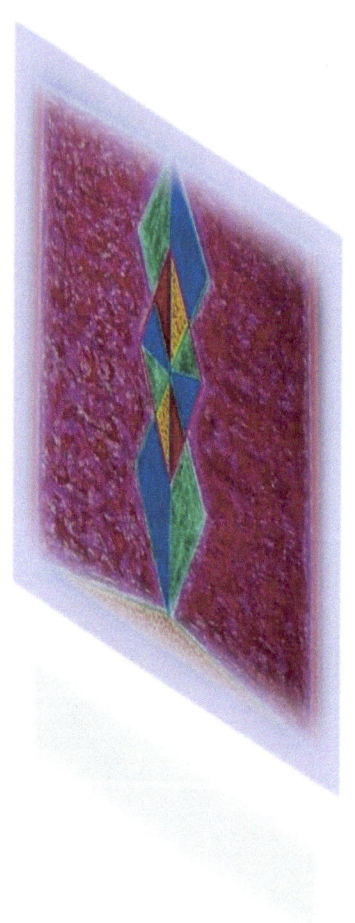

#2

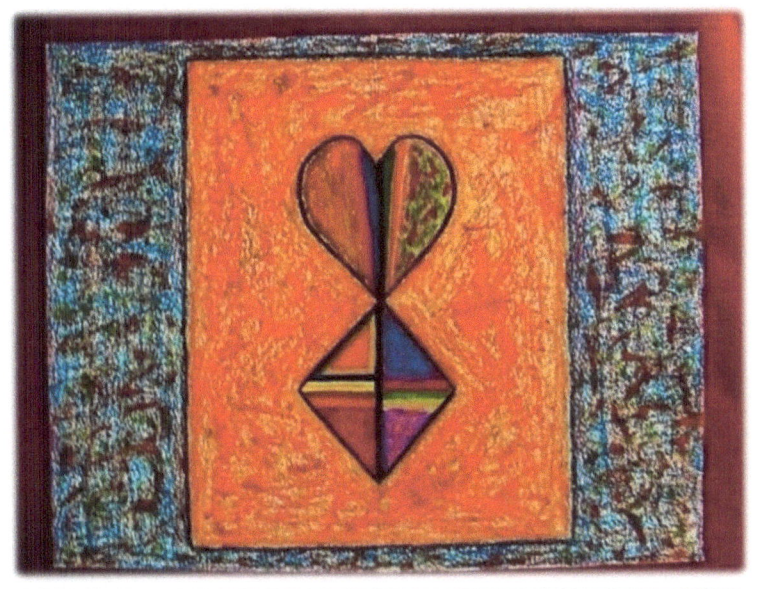

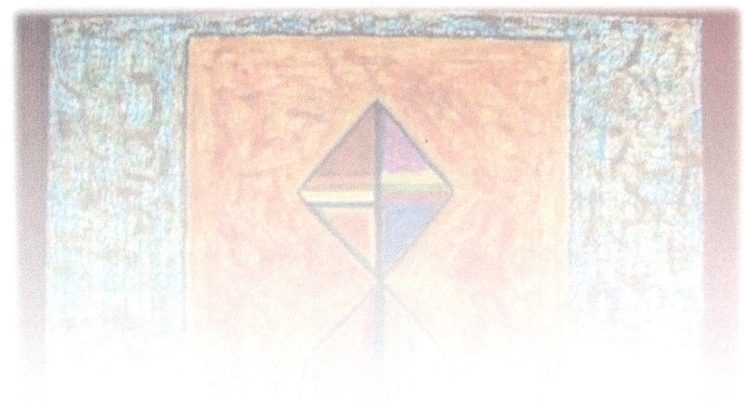

3

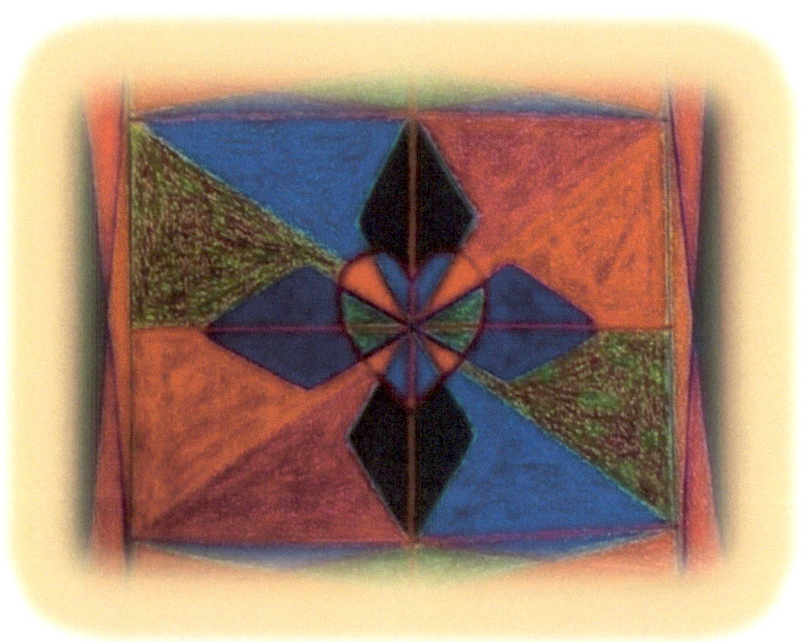

4

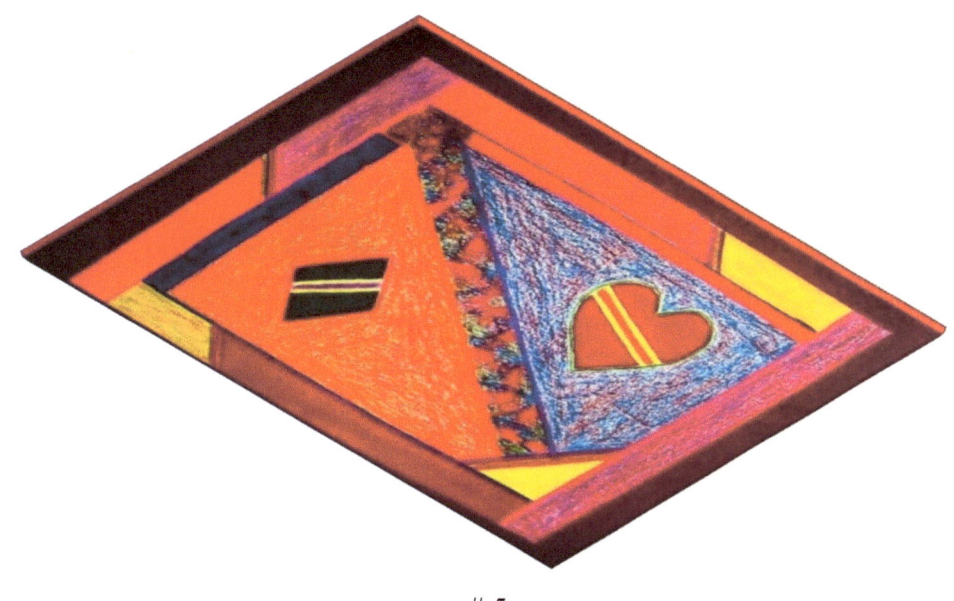

5

Set 3
Pastel Shades
Numbers 1, 2, 3, 4, 5
Colored Pencils & Pastel Coloring & Acrylic Coloring

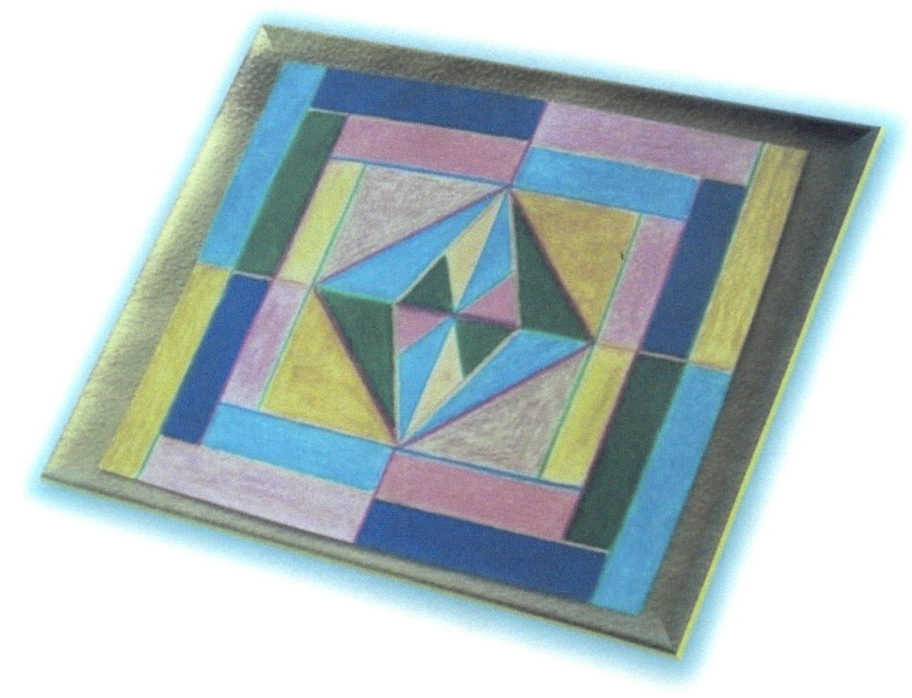

\# 1

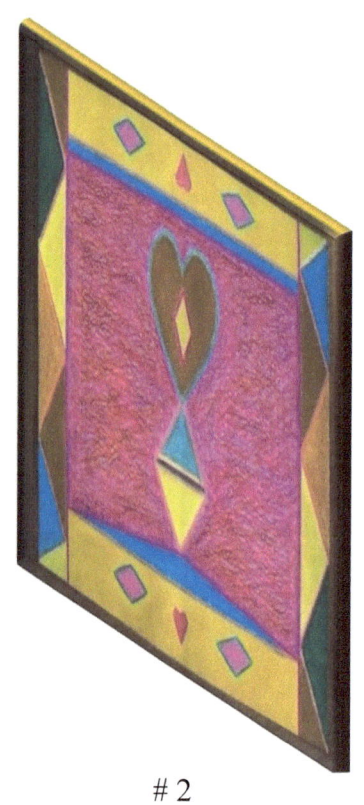

2

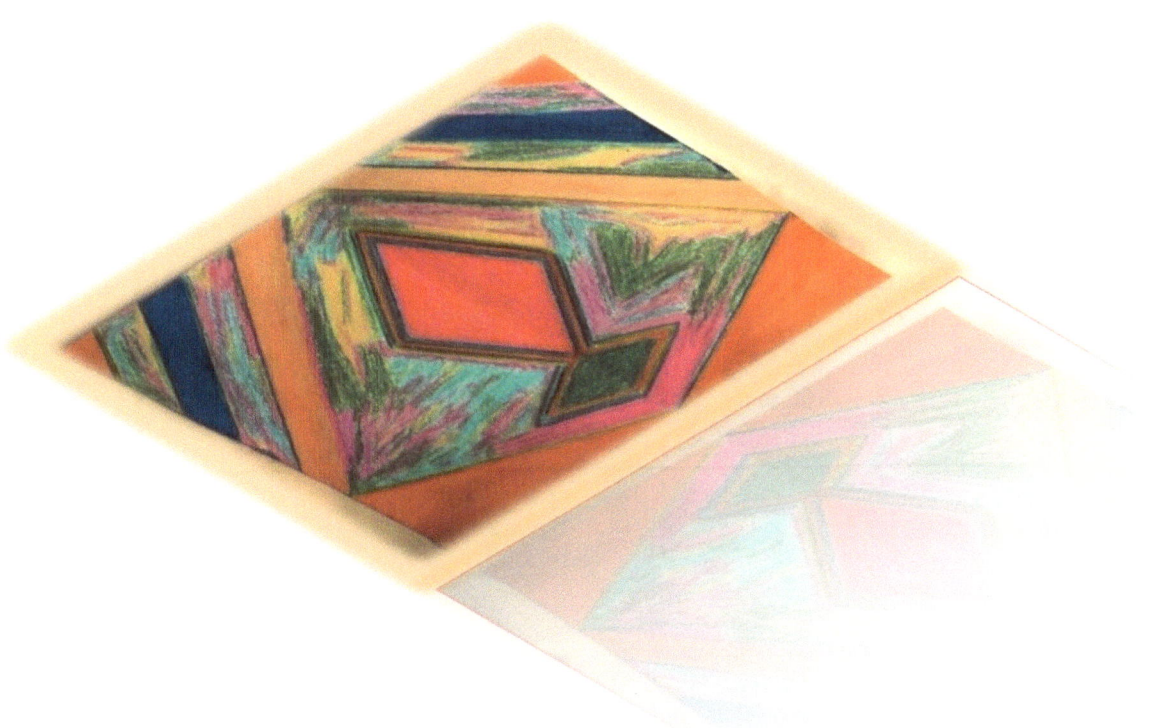

3

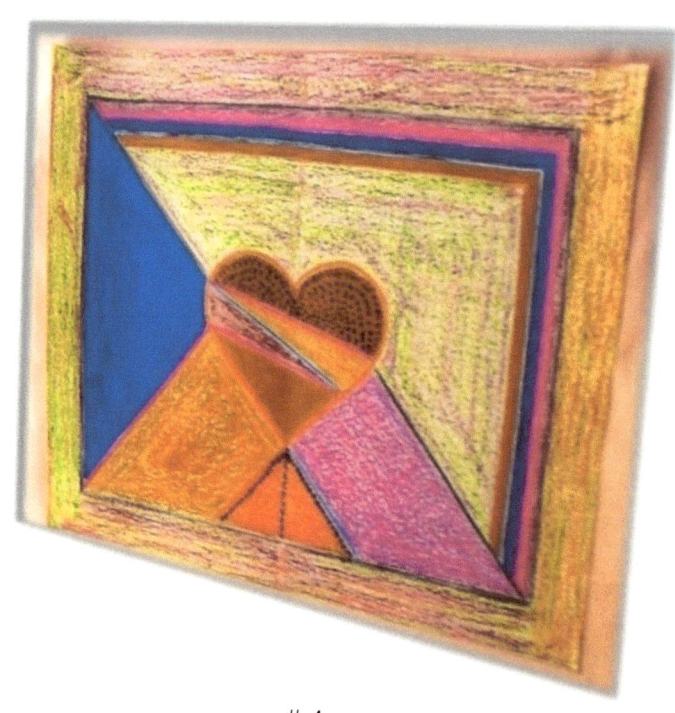

4

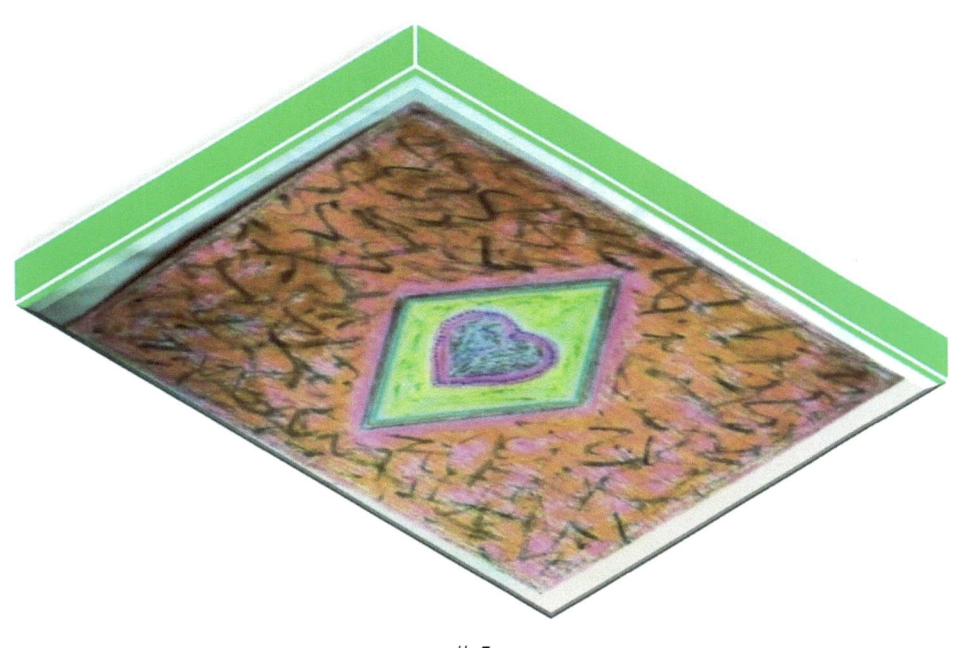

5

Set 4
The Gray, Black & White Diamond & Heart
Art Collection
Numbers 1, 2, 3, 4, 5
Colored Pencils & Pastel Coloring & Acrylic Coloring

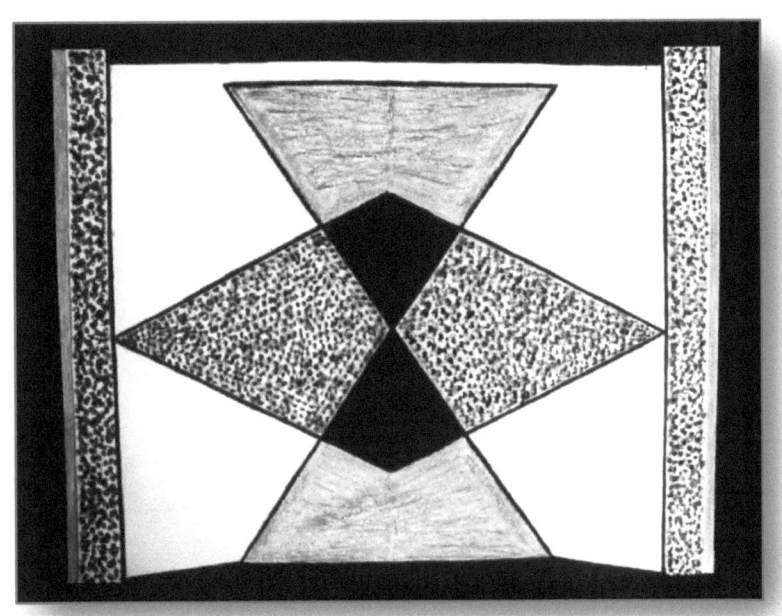

\# 1

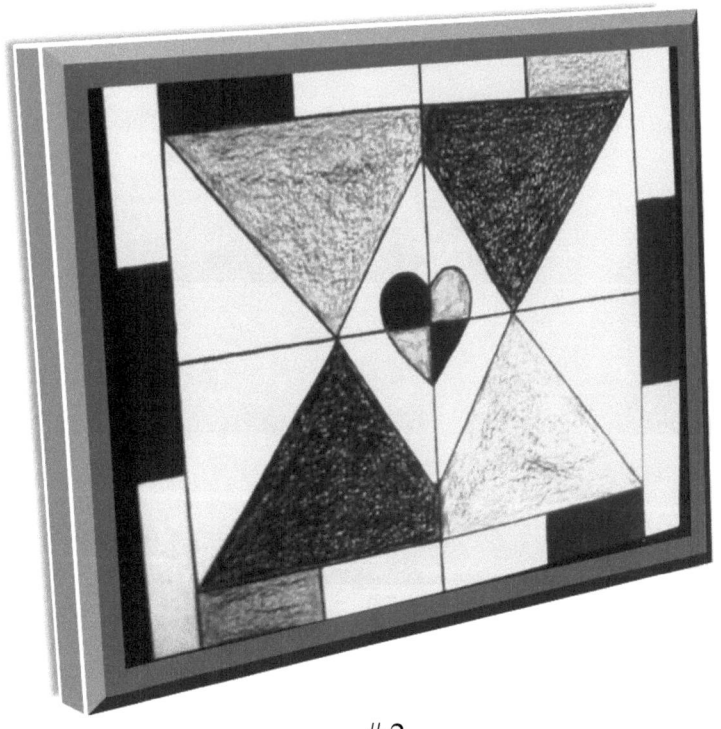

2

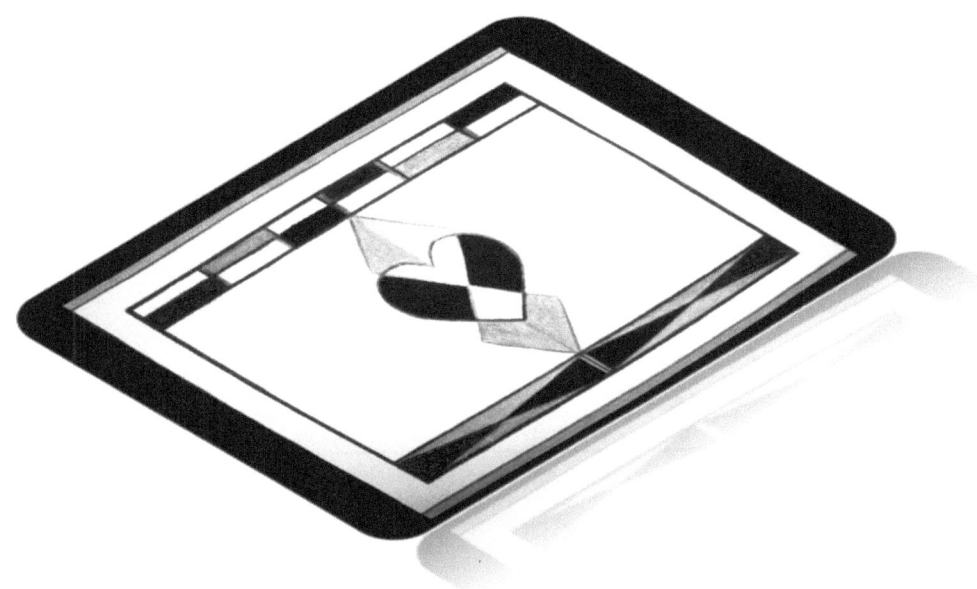

3

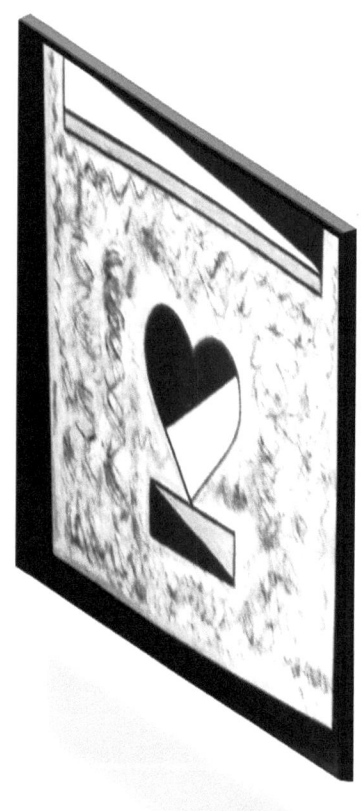

4

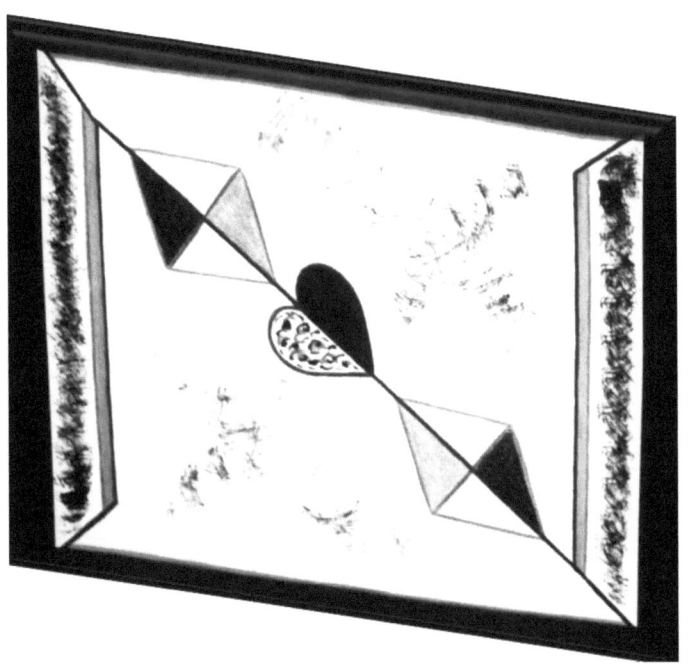

5

Set 5
The Black & White Diamond & Heart Art Collection
Numbers 1, 2, 3, 4, 5
Colored Pencils & Pastel Coloring & Acrylic Coloring

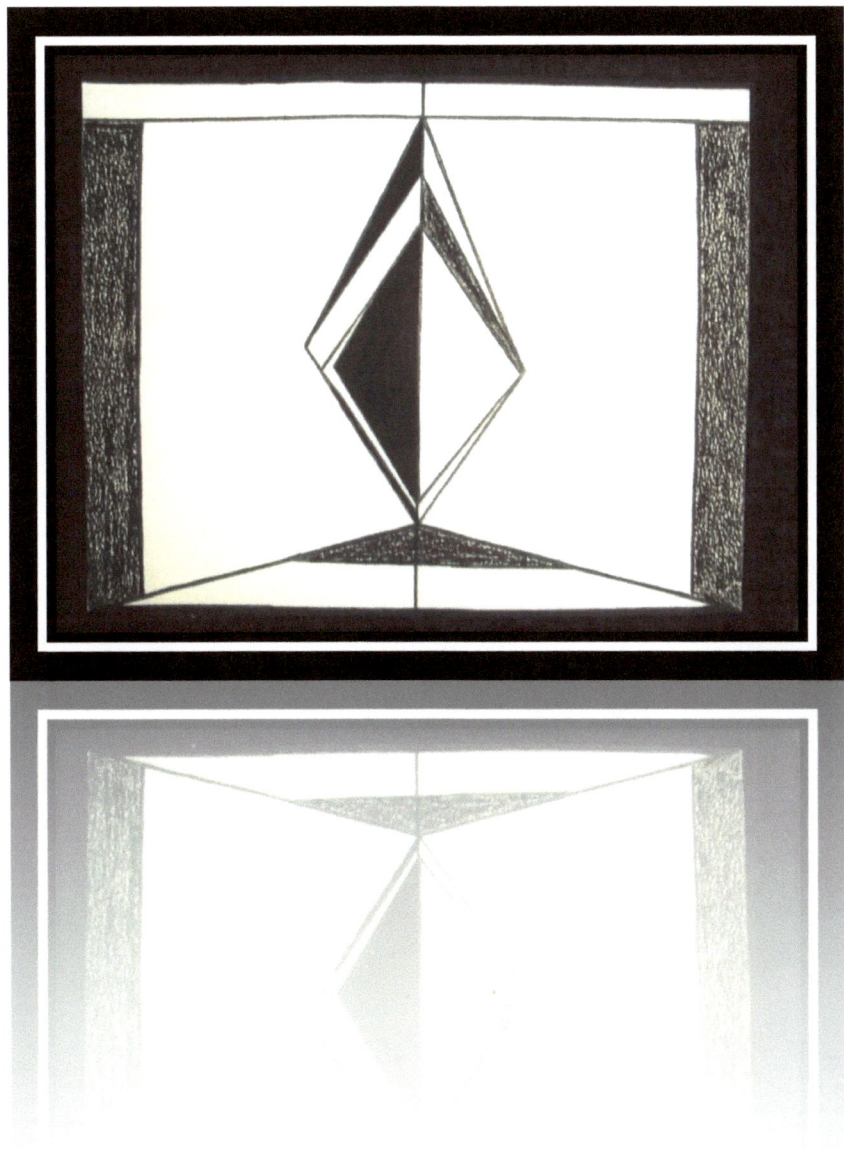

1

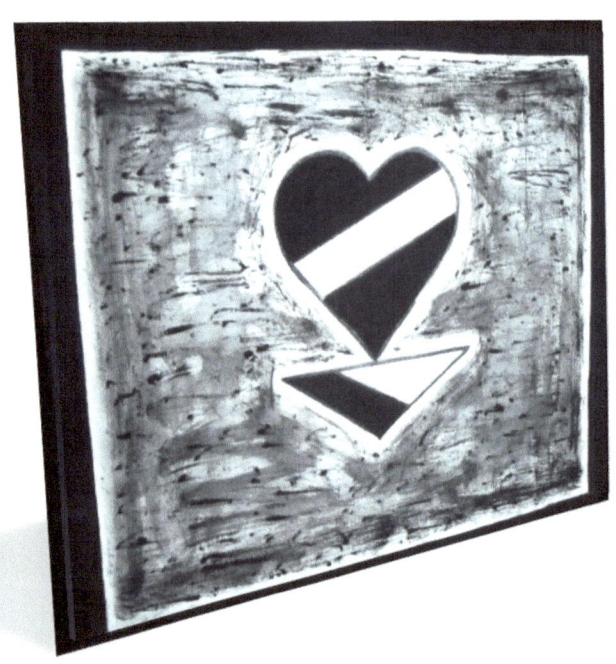

2

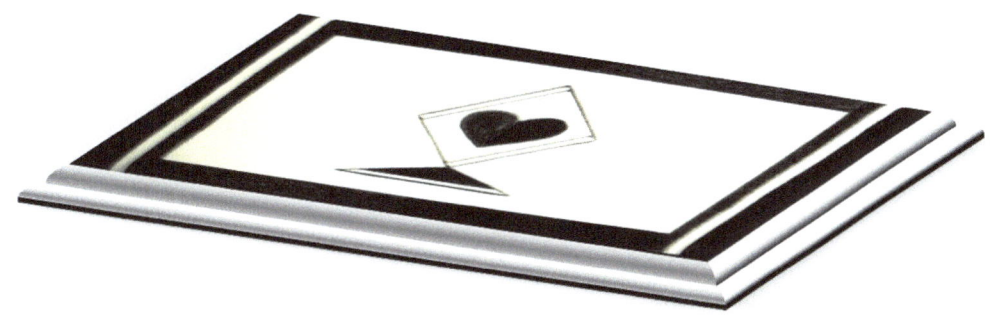

3

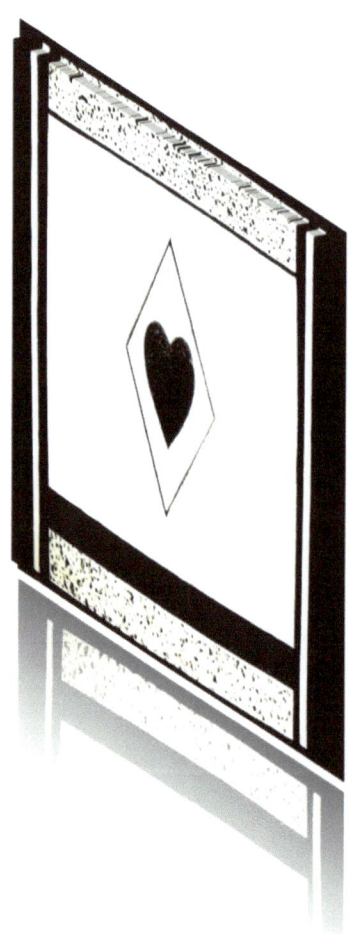

4

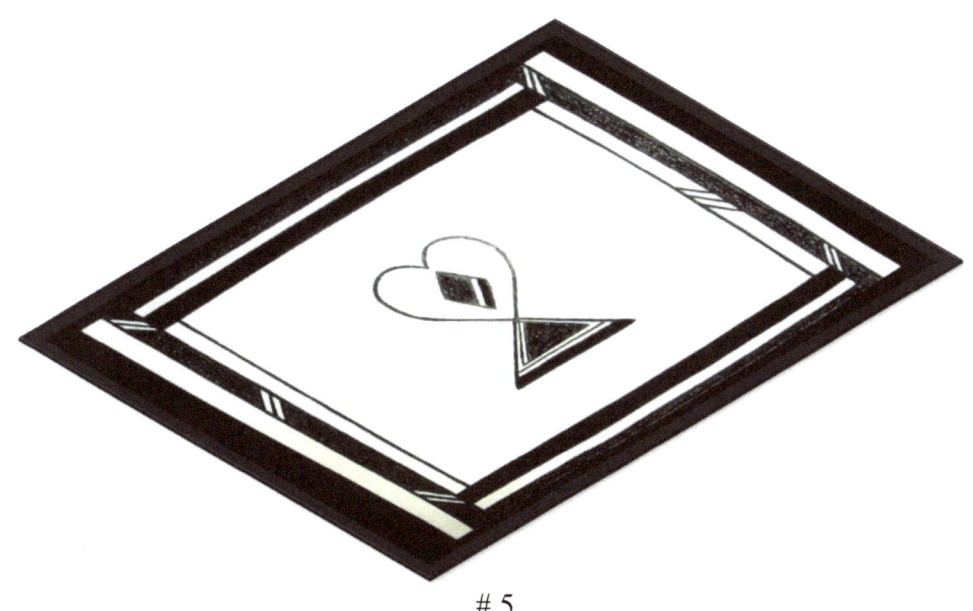

5

Collection III

Set 1

Primary Colors

Numbers 1, 2, 3, 4, 5

Colored Pencils & Pastel Coloring & Oil Coloring

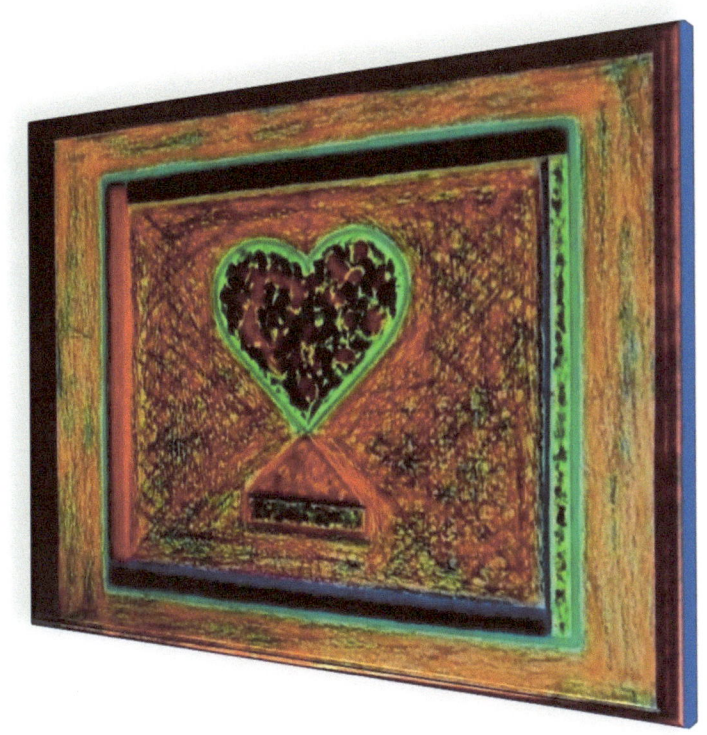

1

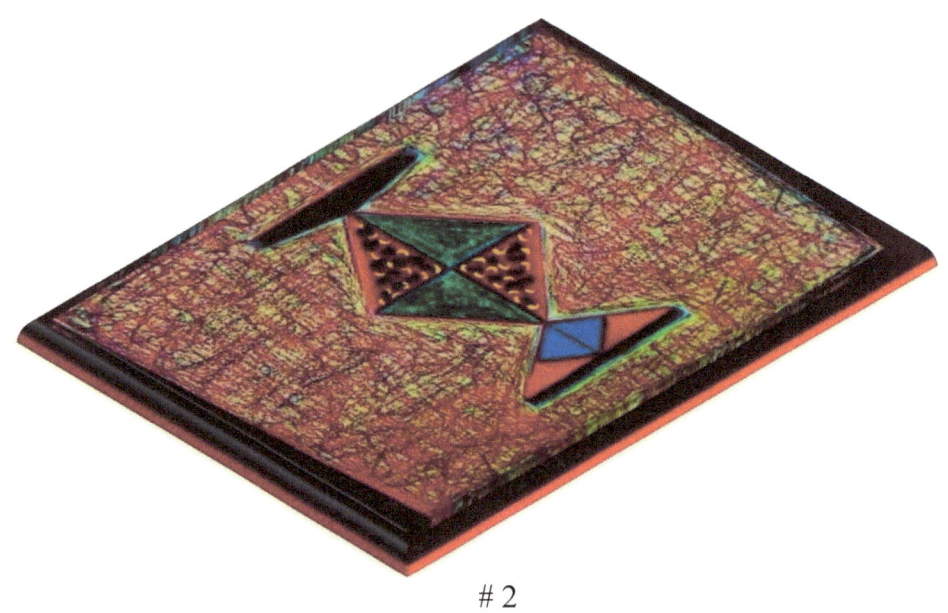

2

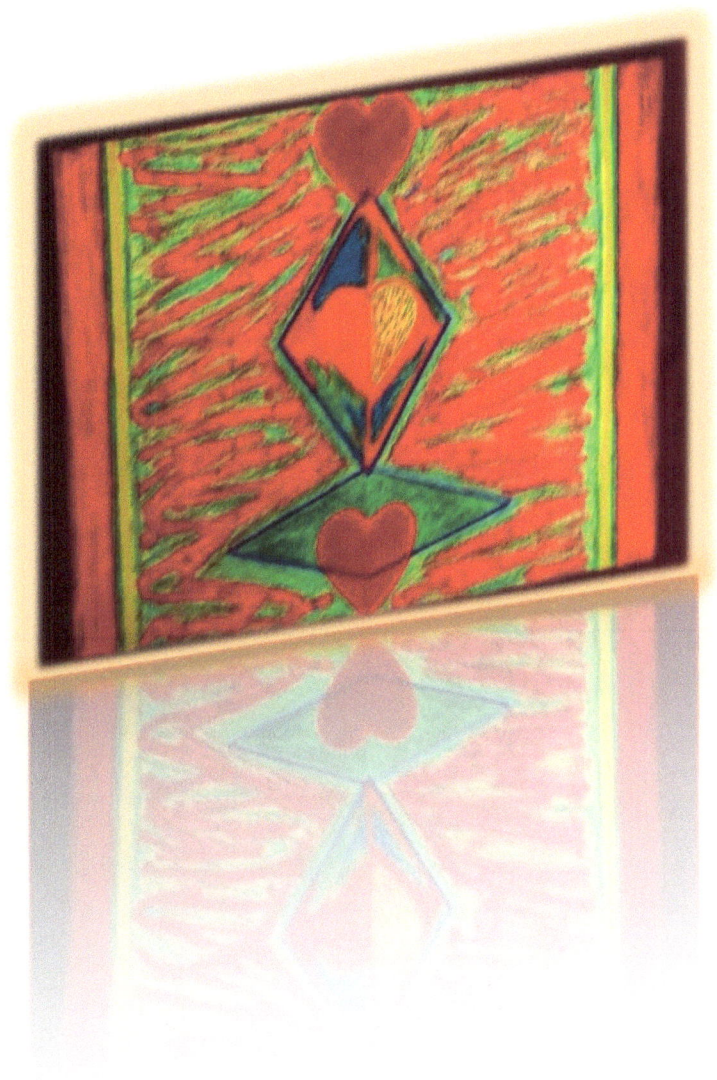

3

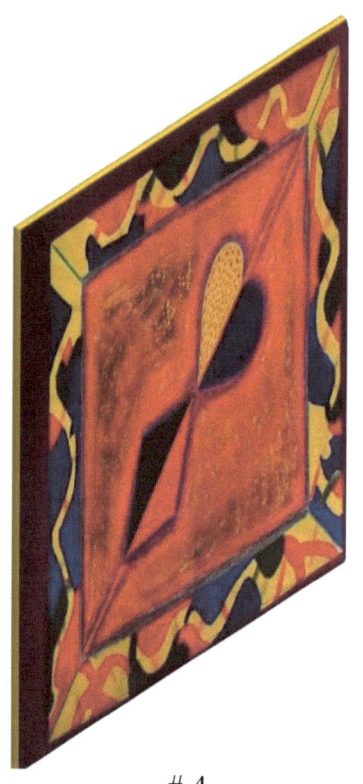

4

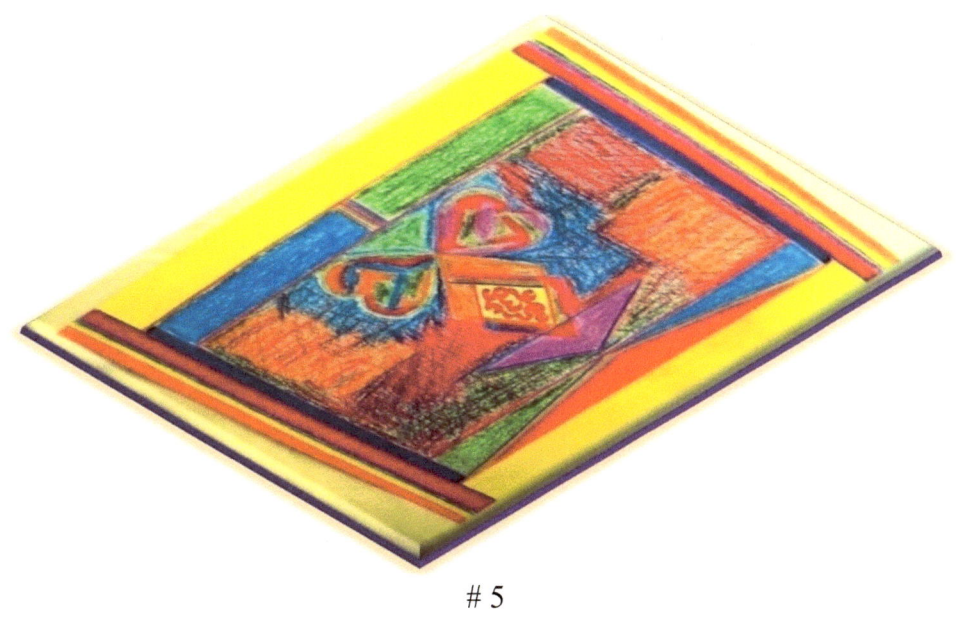

5

Set 2
Pastel Shades
Numbers 1, 2, 3, 4, 5
Colored Pencils & Pastel Coloring & Oil Coloring

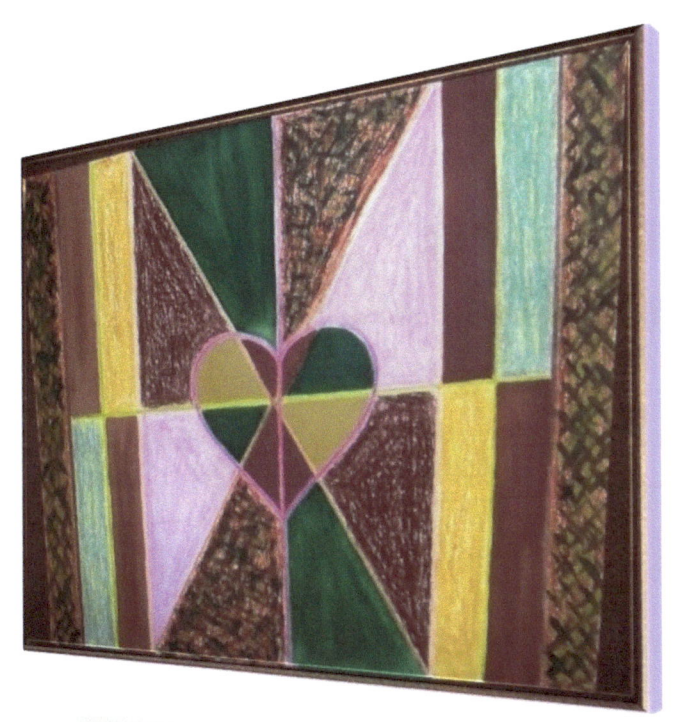

1

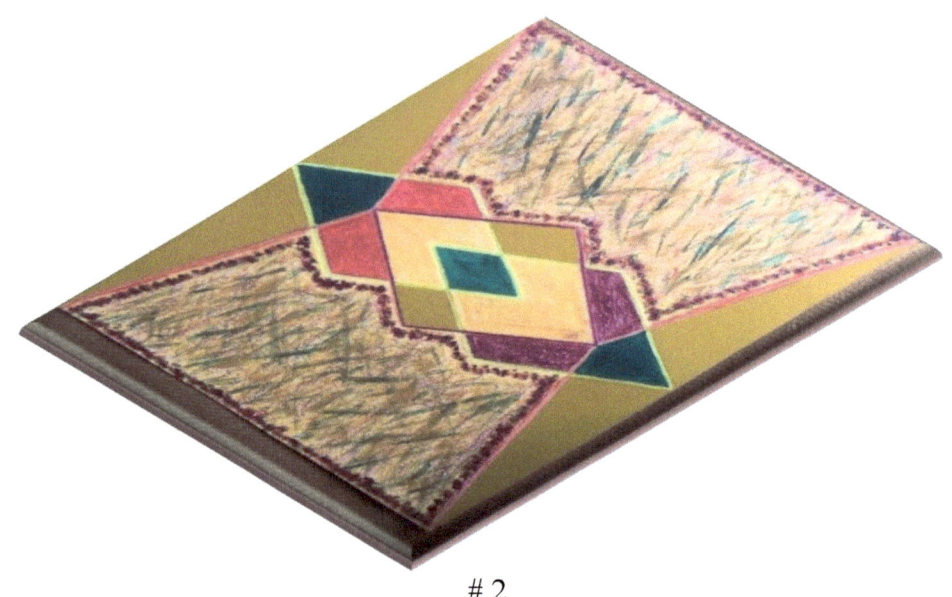

2

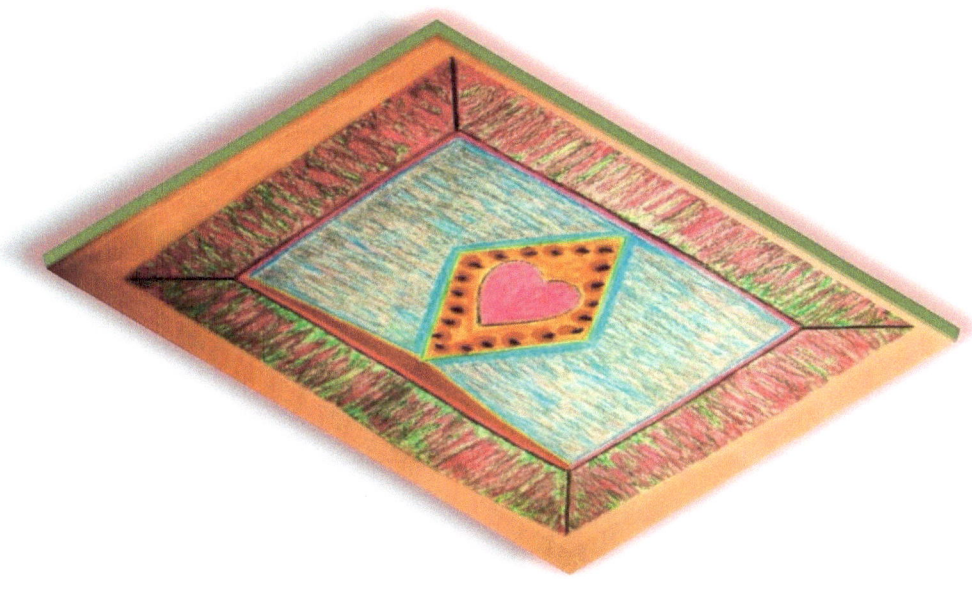

3

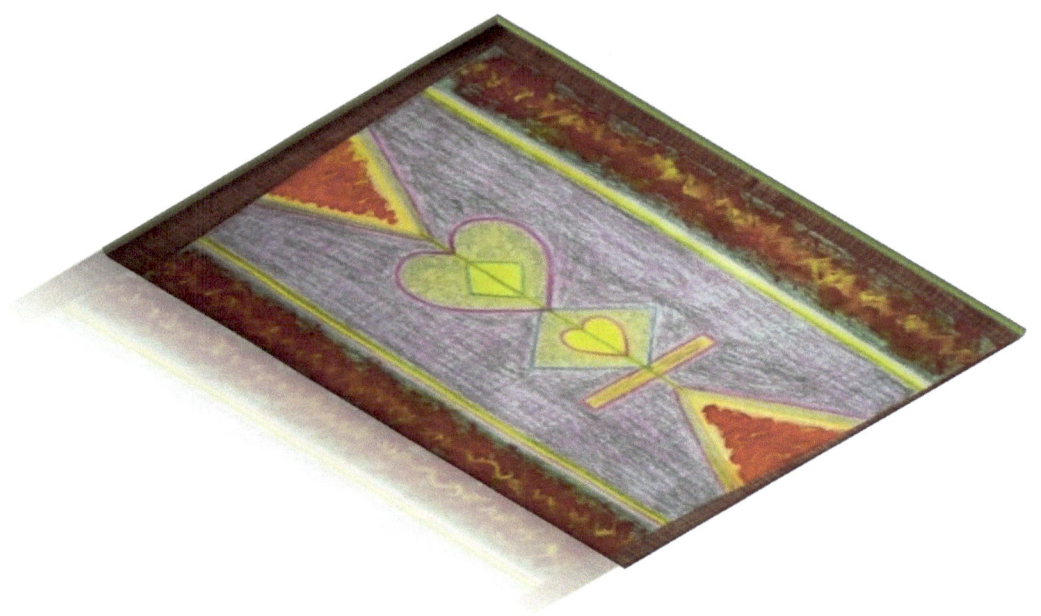

4

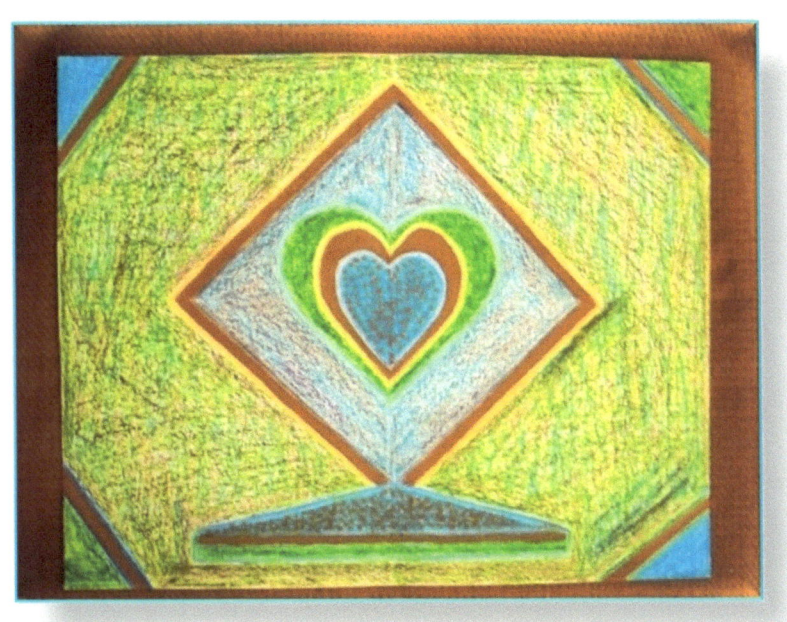

\# 5

Set 3
Earth Tones
Numbers 1, 2, 3, 4, 5
Colored Pencils & Pastel Coloring & Oil Coloring

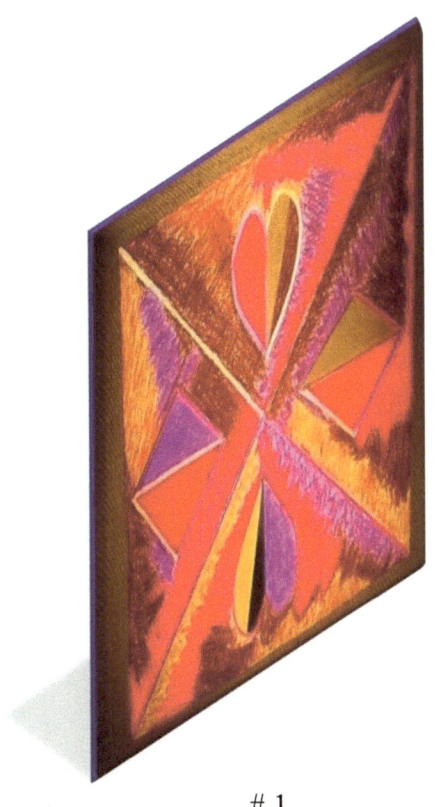

1

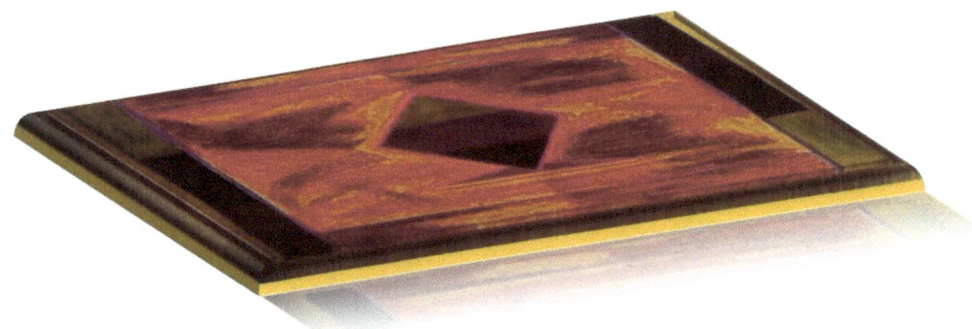

2

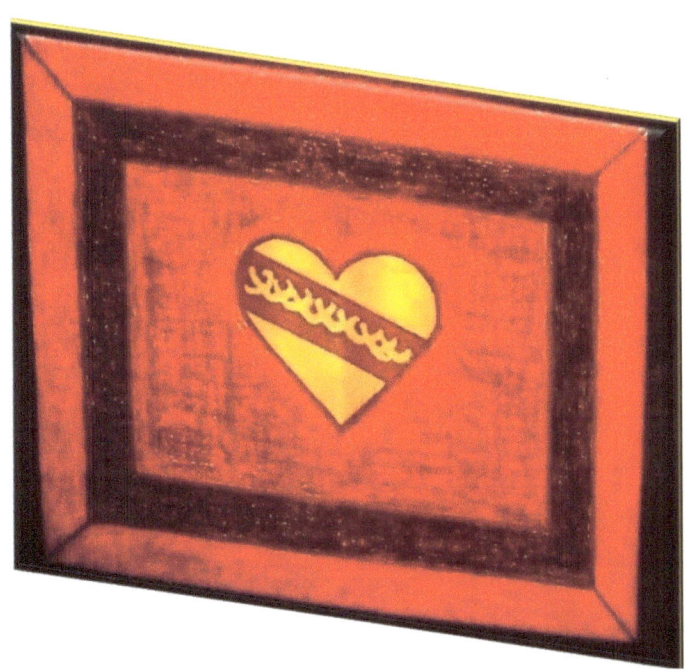

3

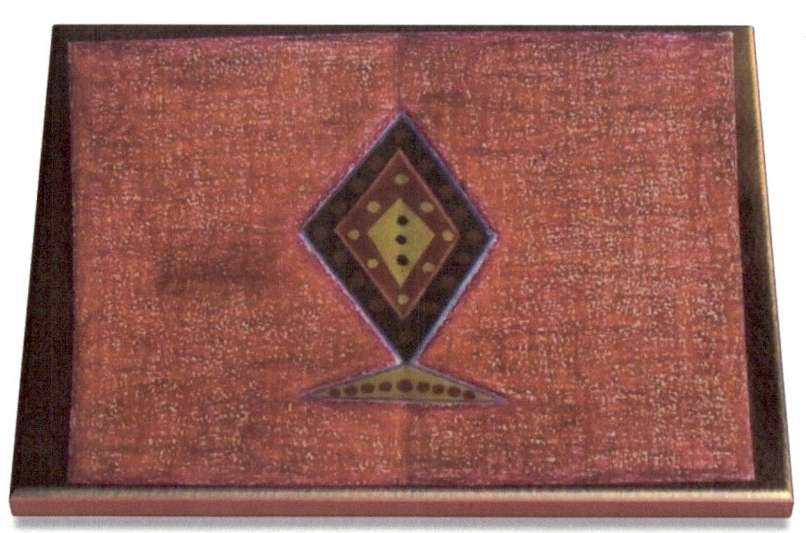

4

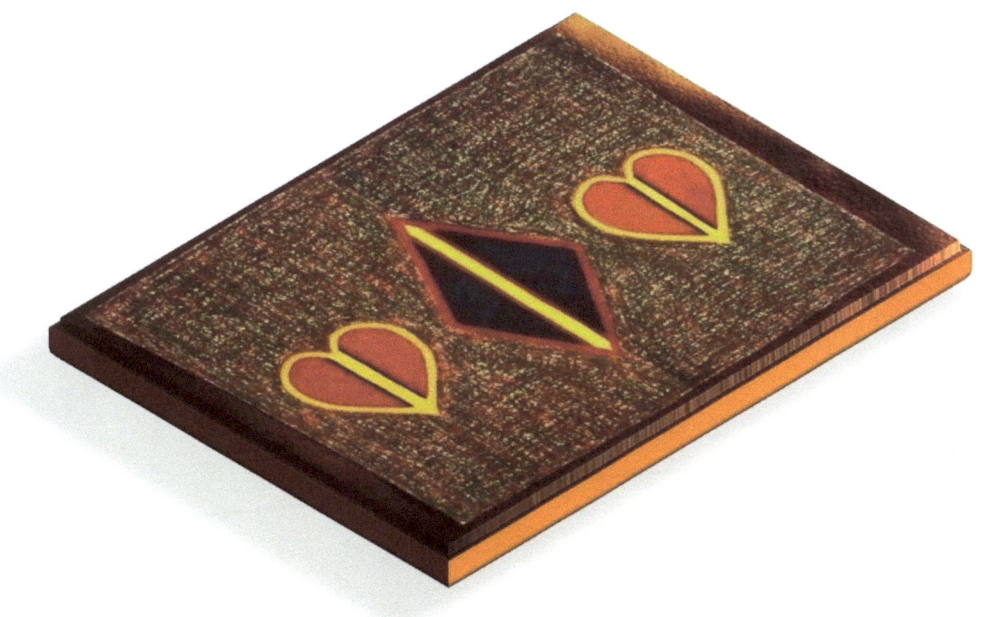

5

Set 4
The Gray, Black & White Diamond & Heart
Art Collection
Numbers 1, 2, 3, 4, 5
Colored Pencils & Pastel Coloring & Oil Coloring

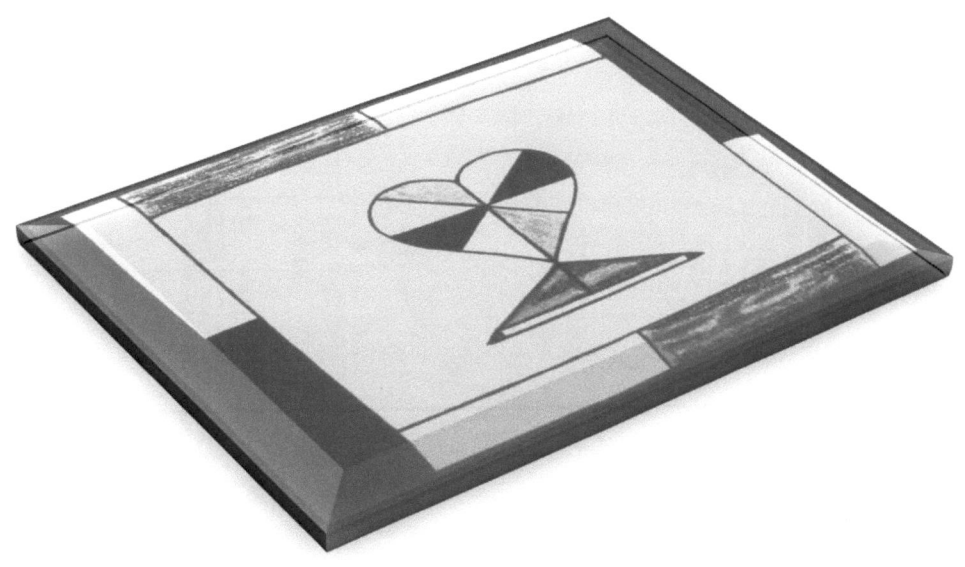

1

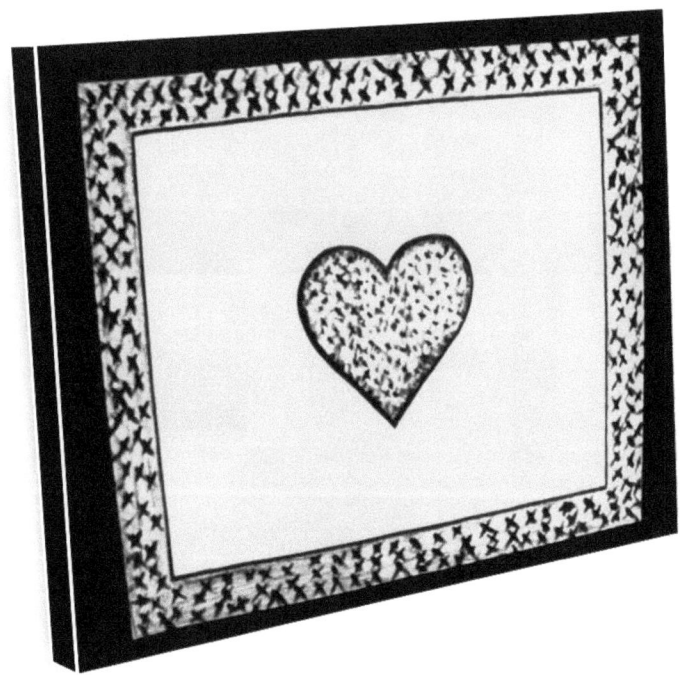

2

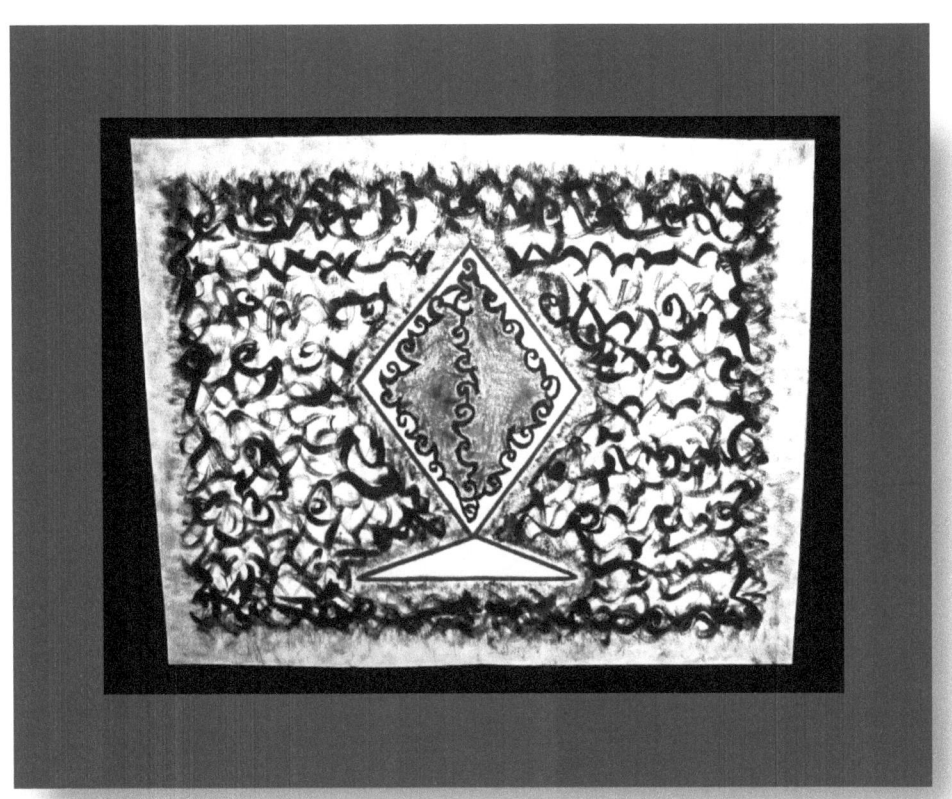

3

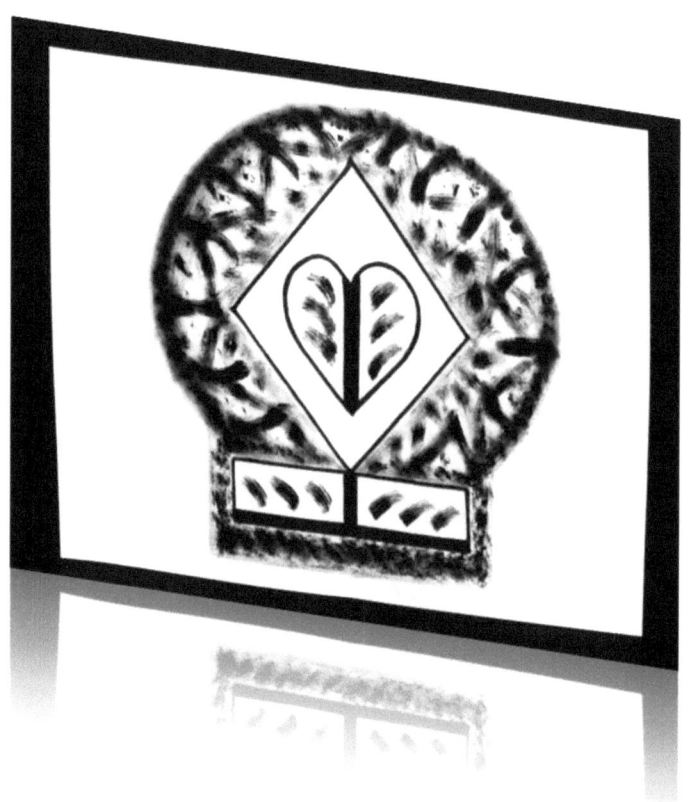

4

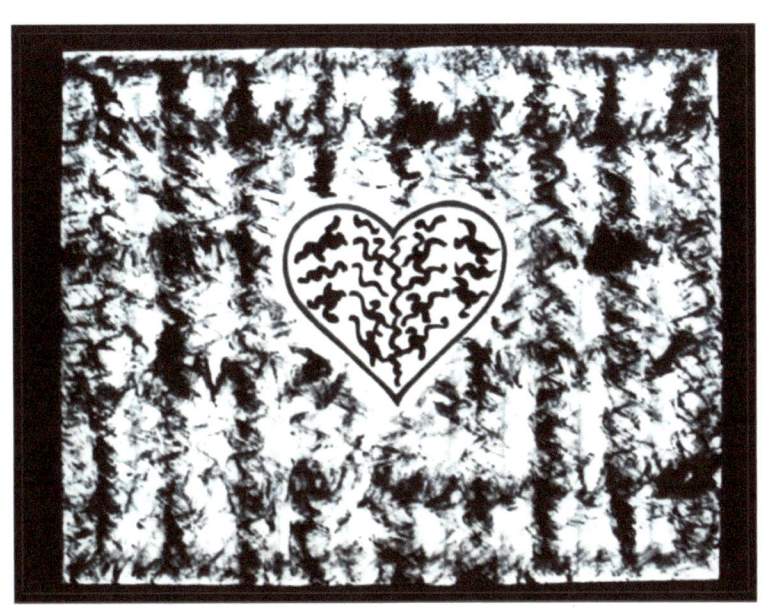

5

Set 5
The Black & White Diamond & Heart
Art Collection
Numbers 1, 2, 3, 4, 5
Colored Pencils & Pastel Coloring & Oil Coloring

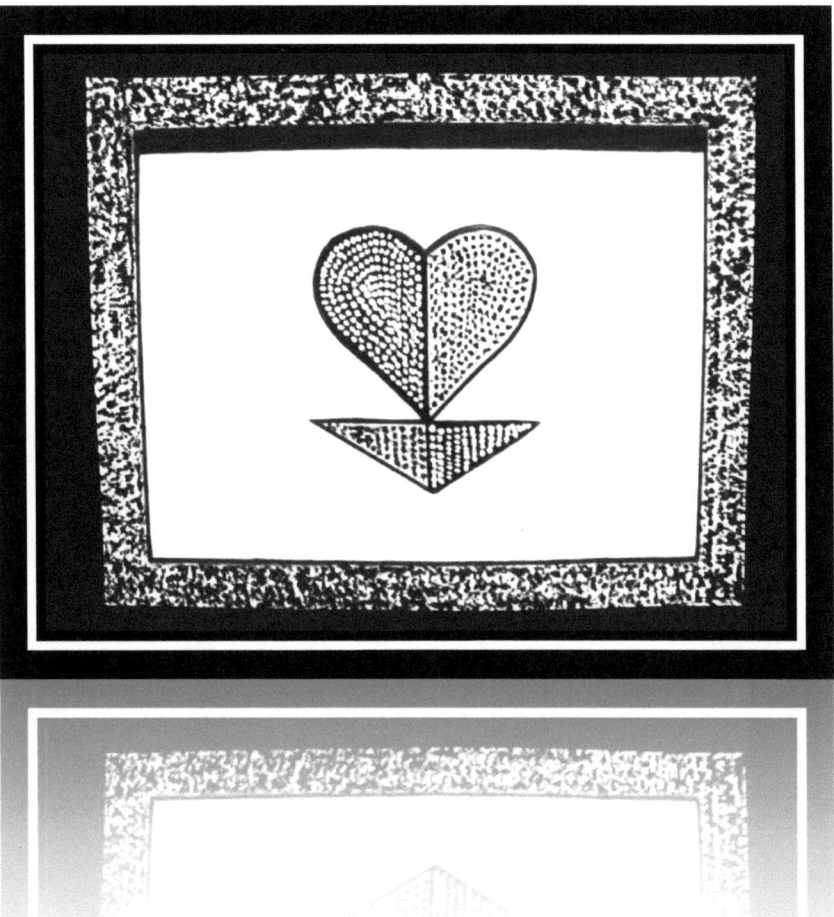

1

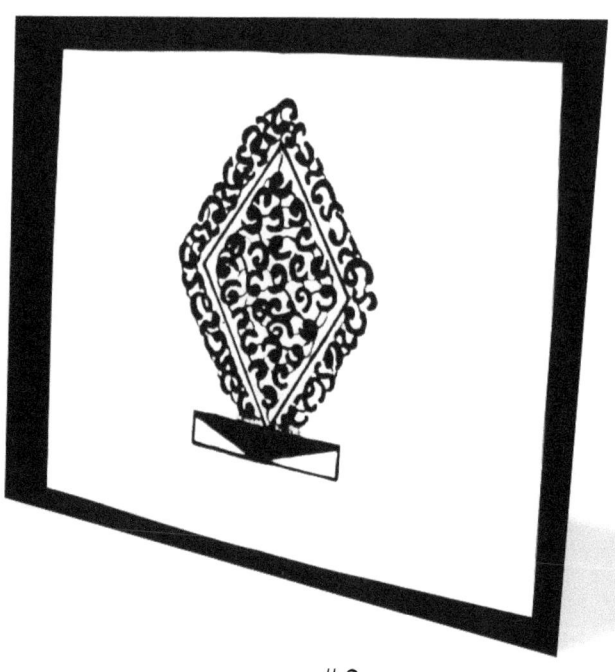

2

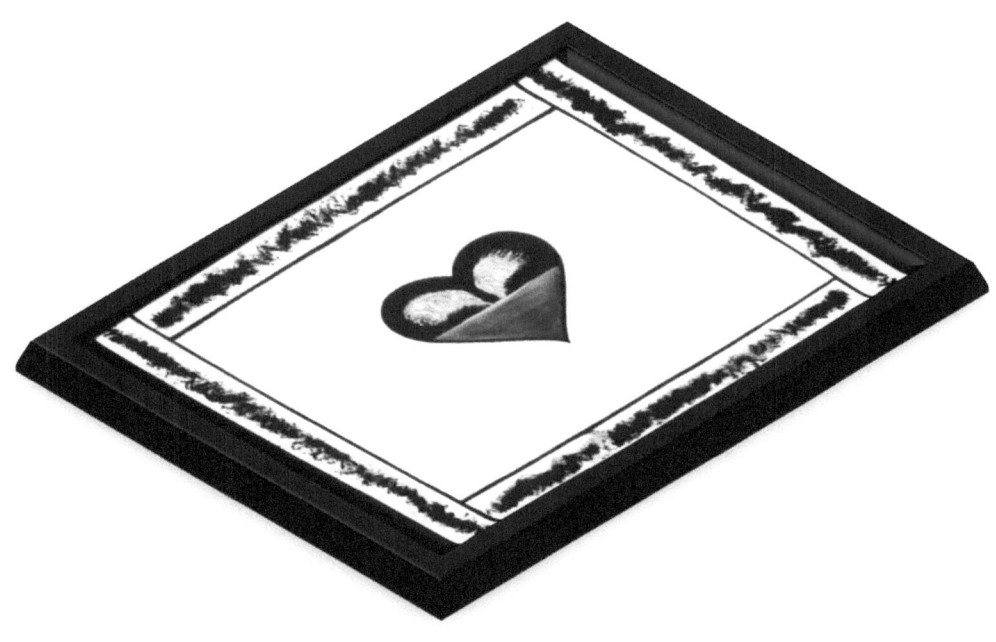

3

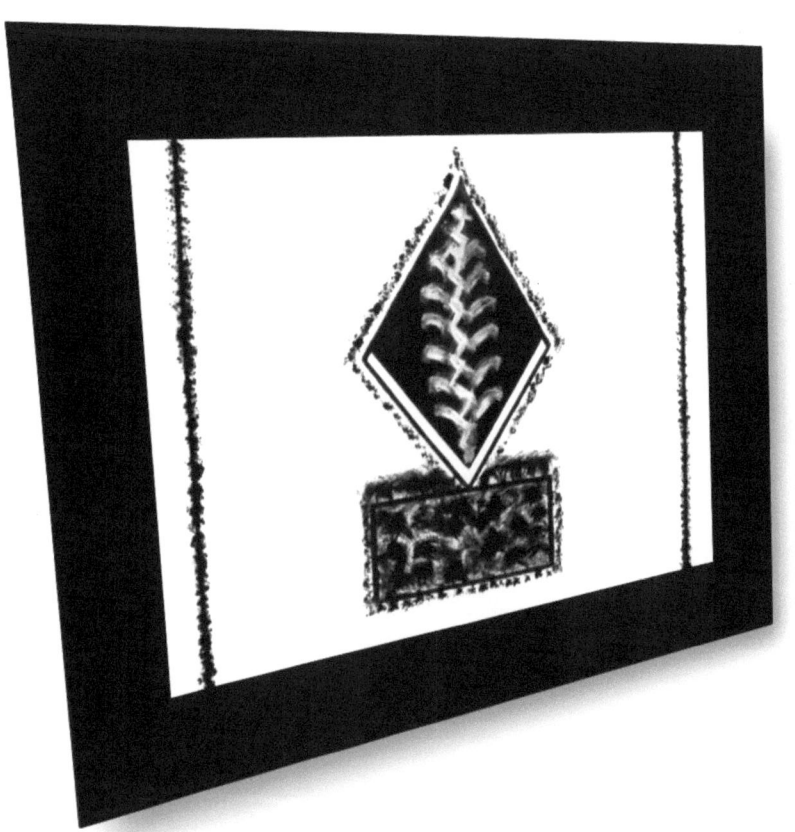

4

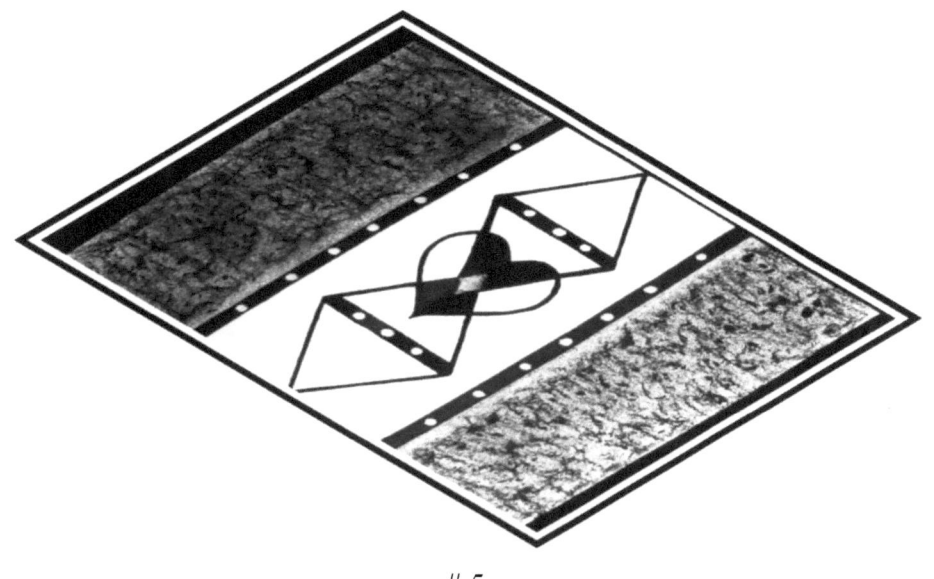

5

The After Picture

I believe whole-heartedly—that, you need not be, so necessarily, an educated, or skillful, nor experienced artist to create art—or, artistry. Rather, you need only to construct a context, in which you know something about its content: terminology; materials; and techniques; and even practices. Then, apply your artistic creativeness to effectuate whatever art work that suits you, specially. Whether it is of Still Life; Figurative Art; Avant-Garde; or, Pointillism; or, even, Clubs and Spades; or, whether you are concerned about *terminology*: texture, dimensions, and the like; or, whether you are concerned about *techniques*: shading and high-lighting; or, cross-hatching; or, even, blending and softening, and so on; or, even, whether you are concerned about stippling, spattering, or, dry-brushing, and so forth; all of which, makes for some interesting if not some fascinating art work—paintings, or pictures.

Especially, if such art work exhibits various *coloring schemes*, (or the mixture thereof): *pastel shades*—aqua, lime, pink, and the like; *earth tones*—brown, tan, umber, and so on; *primary colors*—red, blue, yellow, and so forth; *neutral* or *solid colors*—gray, black and white; black and white; or, *coloring mediums*: colored pencils; water coloring; pastel coloring; plus, acrylic coloring; and, even, oil coloring. But, most importantly, indulge the artistic and creative process or experience, fully. Whereby, you are seeking, so sincerely, some self-fulfillment, if not some self-discovery. Or, seek, and then find the absolutely aspirant artist, whose apt artistry lies, aptly, with-in you; all the while, with-standing any artistry that may not lie within you. Or, better yet, just, become whatever artist that may very well be lying dormant inside of you; even, if you are conflicted, consciously, or, un-consciously, or, even, sub-consciously. Such has been, almost, always, my philosophy of art and the methodology by which I have thus drawn and even painted. And, of course, *best wishes*…!